J. B. Waid

Variety, Poetry and Prose

J. B. Waid

Variety, Poetry and Prose

ISBN/EAN: 9783337372187

Printed in Europe, USA, Canada, Australia, Japan

Cover: Foto ©Thomas Meinert / pixelio.de

More available books at **www.hansebooks.com**

VARIETY,

POETRY AND PROSE,

BY THE

BARD OF NIAGARA.

FIRST EDITION.

Montreal:
PRINTED BY JOHN LOVELL, ST. NICHOLAS STREET.
1872.

TO A

DISINTERESTED FRIEND,

FOR HIS UNMERITED AND CONTINUED KINDNESS TO ME IN THE

EVENING OF LIFE,

AS A TOKEN OF MY REGARD AND ESTEEM FOR HIM AS A

GENTLEMAN AND A CHRISTIAN,

I DEDICATE THIS VOLUME.

I NAME HIM NOT, FOR HIS EXTREME MODESTY FORBIDS IT;
BUT A QUAINT OLD POET, IN THE LINES BELOW, HAS SO
PLAINLY DESCRIBED HIM, THAT FEW WILL FAIL
TO RECOGNIZE THE MAN.

"JUSTLY ARMED,—MAN'S EVERY SIN
ASSAILS DARINGLY; AND MOURNS,
SINCERELY MOURNS, ALL THE HEART'S
EVILS, WRONGS, SORROWS, OR NEEDS,—
EASEMENTS SUPPLYING QUICKLY."

TO SUCH A MAN

I SUBSCRIBE MYSELF HIS THANKFUL AND HUMBLE SERVANT,

BARD OF NIAGARA.

BLEURY STREET, MONTREAL,
JANUARY 1ST, 1872.

CONTENTS.

POETRY.

	PAGE.
Niagara River and Falls	9
Bethlehem's Star	12
A Fable	13
Poems for the times	23
A fragment	28
A wish to a young lady	29
Lines to a lady expected	31
Epitaph on a friend's child	32
God everywhere	33
God the Wonderful	34
God's love seen	35
God's love measured	36
Night	37
On a monumental slab	39
A regret	40
God's will	41
On a mother and her child's stone	43
The flies my little pets	44
Forgiveness	48
Contentment	49
The slanderer	50
To Miss Ellen Mathewson on the death of her mother	52
Earth and Heaven	54
Patience	57
To a co-laborer	58
Weep not, flowers	60
Tedious, tedious	61
A thought	63
The mission of pain	64
Peter's Fall	66
A faithful friend	67
The Bible	68

CONTENTS.

	PAGE.
Cedar and willow gloom	69
Appear before God	71
I would not die	72
God ever near	74
Snug little fire	75
Jesus is mine	78
Is He mine	79
Pure cold water	81
On my only son's tombstone	81
New and old year	82
Birthday	84
A poem on picnic at Bœloeil	85
An adieu to my country	90
To His Royal Highness, Prince Arthur	94
Copy of his letter	97
In memoriam	98
Faith—Hope—Love	100
Be happy	105
Trifles	108
Great things	110
A fragment	113
Whisky devil is his name	114
Impromptu on marriage	115
Bunker Hill monument	116
The three smiles	118
Calvary	119
The fisherman	120
Sabbath School	121
My home	122
Why should you weep?	123
Boys of Switzerland	125
Album kept above	129
On the death of the Hon. T. D. McGee	130
Impromptu on his death	132
The Sabbath	133
To two young missionaries	134
Prisoner of hope	135
The dying year	136
Stream of life	137
Break-heart Hill	138
Let me go	140
Installation Hymn	141
Child and flower	143
To my sister Hannah	144
Go, dear girl	145

CONTENTS.

	PAGE.
On a dear brother	146
Water Hill	147
The returned fair one	149
For an Album	150
Friendship	151
A thought	152
The monument	153
Wish I had never been born	154
New England Conference	155
Another year of toil and care	156
Impromptu on a debate	157
Advice to a lad	158
Temperance song	159
Epistle to my son and daughter	160
A Hymn	165
Consecration	166
On an annual gathering	168
Why not now?	170
The mount of song	173
A riddle	177
Summer's eve	178
Friendship	179
For a monument	179
To a young clergyman	180
My tale is told	181
Israel's captivity and release	184
Hallowe'en, a poem	186
An epitaph	188
Old man of the quill	189
The exile	191
A riddle	194
A verse on a tombstone	194
A reproof	195
The infidel	196
On a friend's monument	197
A widow's thanks	198
Drink the mad'ning bowl no more	199
Death of Rev. G. Pickering	201
The cars of time	203
A hymn, M. E. C.	204
On a father's gravestone	205
Man from Eden wandering	206
The Sabbath school	207
To Mrs. Kezia S.	208
Calvary's fountain	209

CONTENTS.

	PAGE.
Slavery and its abolition	210
And is there a God?	212
To my sister Hannah, a wish	213
Bears or no bears	214
Prophetic, 1832	215
Come, sign the pledge	216
Look not on the dark side	218
Poetic card	219
The California cry	220
Advertisement	225

PROSE.

Five buds it bore	227
Essay	229
Criticism	243
Phrenology	253

BARD OF NIAGARA.

J. G. PARKS, Photographer.

NIAGARA FALLS.

POEMS

BY THE

BARD OF NIAGARA.

NIAGARA RIVER AND FALLS.

Pleasant, peaceful, quiet river,
Limpid, constant, onward ever,
    Gentle waters roll away;
Calm as summer, bright as morning,
Not a look, or sign of warning,
    Naught of danger dost thou say,
But gliding along, mild and strong,
      To the Rapids.
        Then
Sporting, murm'ring, tossing, splashing,
Storming, raving, crossing, dashing,
    Troubled waters fret away;
Hasting, pushing, staving, darting,
Islands mad'ning thee to parting,
    Yet thy tumult cannot stay;
But, tearing along, mad and strong,
      To the chasm.

Then
Curving, bending, bursting, breaking,
Sliding, leaping, rushing, quaking,
 Flying waters dart away;
Flashing, sparkling, wailing, rumbling,
O'er the brink an ocean tumbling,
 To a world of foam and spray,
Fierce shooting along, proud and strong,
 We see thee now
In
Stately grandeur, awful wonder,
Hear thy voice in tones of thunder;
 Falling waters roar away,
Pouring, showering, misting, streaming,
Rob'd in rainbow colors beaming,
 Deck'd by Sol's, or Luna's ray,
Swift plunging along, grand and strong,
 To the bottom.
Then
Foaming, boiling, surging, thrashing,
Breaching, swelling, heaving, crashing,
 Furious waters foam away,
Bubbling, roaring, brawling, curling,
Gurgling, wailing, whisking, whirling;
 Fanciful thy currents play,
Still pressing along, bold and strong,
 Dimpling, pouting.

Then
Gathering, kissing, whispering, hushing,
Panting, smiling, frisking, rushing,
    Lovely waters roll away ;
Winding, eddying, purling, playing,
Lakeward still, and never staying,
    Rustling on thy shining way ;
Free coursing along, calm and strong,
    Soon to mingle
With
Ontario's tideless waters—
Long to be thy prison quarters ;
    Noble river die away.
But I err, a poet's blunder,
Still I hear thy deaf'ning thunder ;
    Here thou art, and here must stay
World-wide wonder, mighty, strong
    Niagara !

BETHLEHEM'S STAR.

'Twas Bethlehem's star of brilliant ray
Which gleam'd upon my darken'd way,
And show'd the fearful road I trod
Was leading far from heaven and God;

Long, long, I struggled with despair;
My spirit felt the touch of death,—
"Save or I perish!" was my prayer—
Uttered as with a dying breath;

That moment burst upon my sight,
The star of pure and liquid ray,
And, like the sun, it chang'd the night
At once into a shining day.

My willing lips the praise shall sing,
Of Bethlehem's Babe, and Zion's King:
That Star of light and truth and love
Shall be my guide to realms above.

A FABLE.—Scene;—Nahant.

Nahant is a peninsula in Massachusetts bay, connected by a narrow isthmus to the city of Lynn.

At the time of writing this poem there stood alone, near by a cavern called "Swallow's Cave," on this peninsula, a Cedar tree, somewhat remarkable for its size and age. This tree was a landmark for the mariner on the coast.

>Just where the cliff o'erhung the sea,
>Near by the Swallow's Cave;
>A tall and ancient Cedar tree
>Look'd o'er the foaming wave;
>
>His branches stiff, his foliage thin,
>An emblem of the past,—
>An aged sire who long had been
>The sport of every blast!
>
>In youth there flourish'd by his side,
>The Maple, Pine, and Elm,
>Whose haughty look and boasting pride,
>Demanded all the realm.
>
>One morning fair while yet the swain
>His heated pillow press'd;
>The Maple with his shallow brain,
>The Cedar thus address'd:

"Ho! withered friend—so old and sere,
Your stay with us is brief;
You cannot live another year
Deprived of sap and leaf;

But, like yon Poplar, wither'd, dead,
A blasted stump you'll stand;"—
So saying, upward toss'd his head,
And flirting mov'd his hand.

The humble Cedar spoke not then,
But listened to the breeze;
Which, rising higher with the sun,
Swep't o'er the boist'rous seas.

It's might increas'd as noon drew near,
And fearful was the blast
Which, through the Cedar's branches sere,
In harmless currents pass'd.

At every gust the Maple groan'd
And bent from side to side,
With pride and shame, he would not own
The fears he could not hide.

Blast after blast with fury came,
Yet firm the Cedar stood;
Submissive, free from fear and shame,
In calm and tranquil mood,—

And thus address'd with modest air
His proud and tembling friend :—
"O that I could your burden share,
And with the storm contend."

"My burden share," the Maple cried,
Mean upstart of the earth ;
If in the ground I was not tied,
I'd make you rue your mirth."

While thus vehemently he spoke,
The wind renewed its force ;—
His trunk unyeilding quickly broke ;—
He lay a lifeless corse!

The wind was hush'd, the Cedar wept
The foolish Maple's fate,
And blessed the hand who safe had kept
Himself and loving mate.

Sol onward mov'd, and night serene
Succeeded to the storm ;
And in her turn night's beauteous queen,
Rul'd till the rising morn.

But ere the lark his matin sung,
Or fisher's boat was seen,
The Zephyr loos'd the Pine's proud tongue,
Who spoke with lordly mein :

"Unsightly being, barren shrub!
Useless to man or brute,
Not fit for axle, shaft, or hub,
Thou ever should'st be mute.

Dost thou presume to proffer aid
When dangerous winds career,
Whose leafless limbs, and trunk decay'd
Bespeak thine end so near?"

As was advis'd by the proud Pine,
The Cedar silence kept;
While round his trunk the tender Vine
With strong affection crept.

The darkness pass'd and golden light
Pour'd from the orb of day;
The wither'd pride, and boasting might,
Before the Cedar lay!

The Vine with sympathy and pain
Spoke of his prostrate form,
Nor could she well from tears refrain,
While musing on the storm.

For, "Cedar dear," she sweetly said,
"My life I owe to you,
Who kindly propp'd my sinking head
When winds so fiercely blew.

If I had clasp'd the haughty sire,
Now withering at our feet,
I soon with him should feel the fire,—
Be ashes, smoke, and heat."

" O grateful Vine, well pleas'd I hear
Those words so kind and true,
I in my turn acknowledge, dear,
The help received from you.

For when the wind with greatest power
Assail'd my upright form,
Closer you press'd me in that hour,
With friendship true and warm."

While thus in mutual embrace
Their hours of pleasure flew,
The Pine and Elm, with scornful face,
Held conversation too.

The Maple, Cedar, and the Vine,
The theme of all they said;
Against the living spoke the Pine,
The Elm against the dead!

No tender feelings mov'd their hearts,
But all was pride and scorn,
With sland'rous words like poison'd darts
They spent the smiling morn.

Meridian rays, like darting spears,
Pierc'd rock, and earth, and plant,
And gently flew the briny tears,—*
Romantic o'er Nahant.

The inland glows with scorching heat,
And zephyrs mildly play;
The orient breeze the zephyrs meet,
And storm obscures the day.

Conflicting winds and clouds are seen
O'er all the troubled sky:
The thunder rolls, and fierce between,
The hail like bullets fly!

Flash after flash with vivid glare,
The zigzag lighting darts,
Astounding thunder breaks the air,
And quails the stoutest hearts!

A little boat in danger's hour
Had gained the friendly cove,
The crew in haste fled from the shower,
For shelter to the grove.

* "And gently flew the briny tears,"—When the waves break with force, even in a calm, on the rocks around Nahant, the spray is thrown at a great distance falling like a gentle shower around.

But one short moment—who can tell
The horrors of that breath!
The lightning scath'd the envious Pine,
And laid it low in death!

The thunder ceas'd, the clouds withdrew,
The boatmen left the strand,
With linen wings they swiftly flew
Far distant from the land.

The sable shroud again was thrown
O'er ocean, vale, and hill;
The twinkling stars, like diamonds strewn,
That shroud with brilliants fill.

The dewy mantle now is spread
O'er sleeping plants and herds,
Man sleeps upon his downy bed,
On branches rest the birds.

No longer could the Vine suppress
The feelings of her mind;
No longer on that bosom rest
With passions thus confined.

She spake,—the Cedar audience gave,
And listened with delight;—
Though solemn as the opening grave,
Her voice broke on the night:

"Dear Cedar when our parent sun
His rays meridian shed,
Beside us stood that lofty one
Who now lies low and dead.

And prostrate on the earth below
His scatter'd fragments lie;
And soon, I fear, our other foe
Must trembling sink and die!

For when the thunder shook the earth,
I listened to the speech
Of seamen, who for shelter fled
Within my tendril's reach.

And when the "Elm," I heard them say,
I hush'd my rustling leaf,
While they agreed some future day,
By yonder dangerous reef

To sink him with a millstone weight *
Beneath the foaming tide;
His naked trunk, erect and straight,
The pilot's eye to guide.

---

* "To sink him with a millstone weight,"—At Lynn the fishermen resort to the expedient of thrusting the trunk of a tree through the hole of a millstone, with the root attached, and then dropping it in the harbor for the two-fold purpose as a guide and a place to moor their boats.

And then alone so high and bleak,
Expos'd, how can you stand,
When now your trunk is old and weak,
And palsied is your hand?"

The Cedar sooth'd the mournful Vine,
And check'd her rising fear;
Assur'd her that his living spine
Would last full many a year;

That Nature's God would him protect—
The seaman's friend and guide—
To mark their way to port direct,
There safe from storm to ride."

Again the Cedar silent stood,
And mute remain'd the Vine;
The morning came, when on the flood
They saw the canvas shine.

The boat approach'd with even wing,
And gain'd the rock-girt bay;
The Elm, unconscious, stupid thing!
Had slept the morn away:—

Nor did he wake, but from the pain,
Which reach'd his very heart,
Giving delirium to his brain,
And to his nerves a smart.

One glance he gave—it was his last—
'Twas to the weeping Vine;—
One pungent thought, 'twas of the past,
Then kiss'd the wither'd Pine!

The glittering steel the deed had done,
Nor branch nor twig remain'd,
And, ere the hills obscur'd the sun,
The waves his trunk sustain'd.

The tender Vine, of social make,
Expos'd to every blast,
Endur'd awhile, then faintly spake,
And calmly breath'd her last.

Alone upon the stormy cliff,
The Cedar now remains,
A beacon to the passing skiff—
Monarch o'er all he reigns!

MORAL.

Ambition, Pride and Envy dies,
While Virtue lives and reigns
Pointing us ever to the skies,
Beyond death's dark domains.

POEM FOR THE TIMES.

Written by request of a large political association in the State of New York and delivered before them in Rochester, N.Y.

Home of our sires—the brightest spot of earth!
We hail with pride the land that gave us birth;
With all her faults we own and love her still;
To make her faultless is our wish and will,
That all the world may wonder as they see,
A nation faultless and a people free.

Our gates are open, and our noble tree,
Whose branches shade the millions of the free,
Spreads forth her arms from the Pacific tide
To old Atlantic, rolling in its pride:
From northern Lakes to Gulf of Mexico,
Her boughs are spread, and still in vigor grow.

Our south and eastern gates—the gates of trade,
Where navies enter, and where fortunes made—
Invite the world, and all may freely come,
Who bring not slaves or worse than slavery—rum;
Our laws, if just, alike would both forbid
And treat importers as was treated Kidd.

Our gates of gold ope to the setting sun,
Where thousands enter and have millions won;
Where Asia's hordes may learn the term progress,
In arts and science, habits, customs, dress.

Our northern gates, from Oregon to Maine,
Are open to Victoria's broad domain,
Where Reciprocity is made the rule,
And he who gains the most, is least the fool.

These all stand open to the oppressed of earth—
Come rich or poor, if blest with moral worth;
Our fields are wide;—come, cultivate our soil,
And reap abundance for your sweat and toil.
Let Erin come, and all the Celtic race;
Here Swede, and Swiss may find a resting place;
Let Greece, and Poland send their thousands o'er;
Hungarians, too, are welcome to our shore.
Come from all climes, oppressed ones, when ye will,
Our vales and prairies with your millions fill.
Bide by our laws, our Institutions learn,
Or leave our shores, and never more return;
For none are welcome to our fair domain,
Who will not that "Americans should reign."
Then bow submissive to the powers that be,
Our country is, and ever shall be, free.

Sons of the sires whose patriot fathers bled
In freedom's cause, and sleep with valiant dead!
To us remain vast duties to perform :
Be valiant, then, and breast the coming storm;
Stand as your grandsires stood, in firm array,
And bleed, if blood is needful to the day ;
When moral weapons fail, and only then,
Can man destroy the life of fellowmen
And not be guiltless by the " higher law ; "
Then sheathe the sword; when justice calls—then draw;
And, like those worthies, never quit the field
Until the foe to conquering heroes yield.

Three mighty powers, as freemen, we must face,
Rum, Slavery, Popery—each our land disgrace;
Each has a marshal'd front extending wide;
If once they rule, farewell our country's pride.
Insult and scorn on us a world will heap,
Enough to make our heroes' statues weep.

This triple foe with triple front we'll face,
Firm, strong, and powerful, each in proper place;
As men of sense, we'll all agree as one;
While aught remains to do, there's nothing done.

Intemperance, first in line, if not in power,
Before our Maine law shall in battle cower;
Though strong and artful is this boastful foe,
Our little Davids soon will lay him low.

The law a sling—the execution stones
Shall bruise his flesh, and fracture all his bones;
Then shall a shout go up from hill and plain,
Who slew his thousands now himself is slain.

Next Slavery, with its fearful front and mien,
"Which to be hated needs but to be seen,"
We meet in field, and, though we struggle long,
We meet to conquer; justice makes us strong.
Wise men may err, good men may sometimes fall,
Many of both does slavery now enthrall,
To conquer then we must on God depend;
Conquer we must for He, His aid will lend;
Then nerve for war, be firm, be bold, be brave,
The fetters break from every suf'ring slave.
"Columbia Hail!" we then with pride may sing
In chorus full, and make the welkin ring;
Our stripes, and stars no longer then shall be
A subject fit for Campbell's repartee.

But see in field another powerful band,
In sacerdotal robes they gravely stand;
Priest, Monk, and Friar, each to act his part,
Christ in their creed and Satan in their heart:
Their plans matured, they act with hellish zeal,
The act alone to us those plans reveal;
But history's page, for many centuries past,
Bespeak to us what we must feel at last,

Unless we wake to action while we may
Indulge a hope that baleful power to stay.
Could we but see the fearful plan that's laid
By Pope, and Priest, our sacred rights t' invade,
There's not a man, though lethargic before,
Who would not haste to join our battle corps,
And be prepared to meet in open field,
This hellish foe, with hellish plans, concealed—
Foes to our sacred Institutions all,
Who hope to see our proud Republic fall,
That on the ruins of our blood-bought home,
May rise a Despot, he, the Pope of Rome!

The trumpet sounds—it is our country's call;
We haste to battle with those giants tall,
We'll nail our eagle banner to the mast,
Leonidas like we'll fight unto the last,
Rather than yield to such ignoble foes,
Who now our rights, and liberties oppose.
With three bold fronts in one united band,
We'll meet those foes, and firm as truth we'll stand,
We'll meet—we'll conquer—by the help of God,
And tread the path our conquering fathers trod.

Our council fires we'll light on every hill,
To call our warriors from the field and mill,
From bench and bar, from counting room and boat,
All armed with weapons tried—a "Freeman's vote."

Our central fire shall cast its light quite o'er
The United States, and shine from shore to shore,
Emblem of him who was our nation's sun,
The noble, glorious, hero, Washington;
We'll call, as he call'd on the good and great
To rule our land, and wisely guide our state.

A FRAGMENT.

'Tis spring, drear winter's reign is broken,
    The buds put forth, the bloom's unfolded,
Each tree and bush gives ample token
That Nature's God in power hath spoken,
    And has with plastic hand remoulded
Embryo fruits in Nature's womb,
And life call'd forth from Nature's tomb.

A WISH TO A YOUNG LADY.

I wish you a :—
    Neat little cottage, on a nice little farm,
    Well finished, well furnish'd, convenient and warm;
    Not far in the country, nor on the sea shore,
    But handy to market, the church, and the store.
    A kind pretty husband, and not very old;
    Genteel in his manners, not fearful or bold;
    Not pleased without reason, nor vexed without cause,
    Acquainted with logic, religion, and laws;
    A trade, or profession, it matters not which,
    If gold he has plenty, and always is rich.
    Choice servants I wish you, kind, cleanly and true,
    Who will not complain till there's nothing to do.
    A spring of good water both constant and clear,
    With wood a great plenty piled up for the year.
    A chaise, or light carriage to ride into town,
    Well covered, well painted, red, yellow or brown.
    A horse, or a span of Arabian breed,
    High mettled, yet gentle, excell'd not in speed.
    A driver so careful you need never fear,
    Though swifter you move than the ostrich or deer.
    An orchard of fruit, and a garden of flowers,
    Where you and your husband may spend happy hours.

A lib'ry select, of books, old and new,
Which days would not number, a lifetime read through.
And all kind of fixtures for pleasure and ease,
Which you at your leisure may name if you please.
With these, and good friends, and good neighbors to boot,
Not a day, nor an hour could Hannah be mute,
But you'd hear from the parlor, the garden and wood,
The song of contentment and sweet gratitude.
To close my good wishes, I wish you may find
The "Pearl of great price" which enriches the mind,
A treasure so costly, so brilliant and rare
It cannot be kept without watching and prayer.

LINES TO A LADY EXPECTED.

"Yes, loving is a painful thrill,
And not to love more painful still,
But oh! it is the worst of pain
To love,—and not be loved again."

I love thee Judith, good and kind,
I love thy truthful, noble mind,
I love thy features, smile, and voice,
I love, and choose thee—grant my choice.

No other will I ever choose;
Without thee, all earth's bliss I loose;
My hope—if mine—if not despair
May end a weary life of care.

Be good, my Judith, O be good,
And feast thy soul on angel's food,
On sacred love, divine and pure,
Which makes eternal bliss secure.

Be wise, my Judith, O be wise;
Choose that which leads thee to the skies,
If pure, there we shall reign and sing;
With Christ our Prophet, Priest and King

Be blest, my Judith, O be blest;
This earth is not our place of rest,
Though happy here, if good and wise;
Thrice happy where our treasure lies.

My wish shall be my constant prayer,
With Judith, earth and heaven to share,
And feel the bliss while here below,
That thou art mine in joy and woe.

AN EPITAPH ON A FRIEND'S CHILD.

Nipped by the frost of death, the flower
Hath been transplanted in the skies,
And blooms forever in the bower
Where ne'er a single blossom dies.

GOD EVERYWHERE.

God is here, say the stars as they twinkle on high.
God is here, says the sun as he rolls up the sky,
God is here, says the moon as she waxes and wanes,
God is here, says the comet, and there, too, He reigns,
Where, long centuries since, I wandered so far
That the moon disappear'd and the sun was a star.

God is here, says the mount when the volcano broke,
And here, says the lightning as in thunder it spoke,
God is here, says the river as onward it flowed,
God is here, says the wind as more fiercely it blowed,
And is where I first spread my invisible wings,
Ere yet there were mountains, or rivers, or springs.

God is here, says the ocean while rolling in might,
God is here, says the darkness, and here, says the light;
God is here, says the cavern in stillness profound,
And here, says the earthquake as it upheaves the ground,
Then I heard, in one voice, all creation declare,
He is here! He is here! He exists everywhere!

GOD THE WONDERFUL.

See we wonders, is there aught else
In the sky, the earth, the main,
In the dew-drop, in the planet
In the lightning, wind and rain?
Astounding wonders all may find,
Through matter up to subtle mind.

Greatest wonder, He who made all,
Gave to everything its place—
Stellar systems, planets, comets,
Arch cerulean deck'd with grace
To man, His masterpiece, the earth—
Greater than its wealth his worth.

Shall man's mind, however great 'tis,
God to comprehend aspire?—
Greater than a God he would be,
While indulging such desire;
Comprehender must be greater,
Creature higher than Creator!

Humbly let us God submit to,
Bow adoring at His throne;
Laud His wonders as we view them
Widely through creation strown;
With all our wondrous powers adore,
The Wonderful, and doubt no more.

GOD'S LOVE SEEN.

'Tis seen in every twinkling star,
In sun, and moon, and planets all,
In comets as they wander far,
In brilliant meteors as they fall,
In mountains, rivers, rocks and hills,
In field, and fountain, bush, and tree,
In lakes, and brooks, and purling rills,
Earth, air, and sky, and sea.
'Tis seen in darkness, and in light,
In storm, and sunshine too,
In hail, and rain, and lightnings bright,
In snow, and mists, and dew;
No object on this rolling ball,
Or in the orbs above—
To vast creations outer wall—
But says that "God is Love."

To learn how vast that mighty love,
Behold God's only son,
In Gethsemane, on Calvary,
Crying "Thy will be done!"

That WILL our fallen race to save
From sin and endless woe,
His only Son He freely gave,
That boundless love to show.

GOD'S LOVE MEASURED.

God so loved the world that He gave His only begotten Son, &c.

I find it in my heart to sing
A hymn of praise to Zion's King,
For all the wonders of his grace
Bestow'd on us, a sinful race,—
To cheer us in our dark abode,
And guide our steps to Zion's road.

Lost! lost! indeed was ruined man,
So lost without a heavenly plan
He ne'er could gain the King's highway,
But on in error's path must stray
To ruin's brink, and headlong there
Plunge in a gulf of dark despair.

But Bethlehem's star, with liquid light,
Dispelled the shades of nature's night,
And showed the pathway all have trod
Who now surround the throne of God.
O what a debt of love we owe
To God, who lov'd His creatures so,—

To give to us His only Son
To die, and say " Thy will be done!"
To die for sin, who knew no sin,
And with such love our hearts to win,
For this let all within me raise,
To Him a constant song of praise.

NIGHT.

"An undevout astronomer is mad."—Young.

Who can go forth at night and gaze
On all the wonders of the star-deck'd sky,
And render not the heart's adoring praise,
To Him who placed those shining orbs on high?

Who can peruse that page of light,
And read not there, "There is a God" of love,
Of wisdom infinite, of awful might,
At Whose command, in order, planets move?

See where the sun hath sunk to rest,
While twilight reigns in mingled night and day;
Dimly, and seldom seen, now cheers the west,
The planet Mercury on his shining way.

Next Venus, in her robe of white,
Walks forth, the beauty of the shining plain.
Then war-clad Mars sheds forth his crimson light,
And younger planets follow in his train. *

---

* "Younger planets." The Ataroids of which there are many now discovered, more than a hundred.

Peerless, with his attendant four,
In pearly light, great Jupiter appears;
In pomp he moves his lengthened circuit o'er,
And measures his with twelve of earth's short years.

Pale Saturn next appears in view,
With eight moons, and circling zones of light;
And, ere he passes his long journey through,
Three tens of solar years shall mark his flight.

Next in the train fair Herschel shines,
With his six moons along his distant way;
With four score years and four, he his defines,
And faintly sheds to earth his borrow'd ray.

Leverer's telescopic ball,—
"Neptune,"—with scores of Saturn's years in one,
Plainly deriving, as do planets all,
Light, heat, and color from the distant sun,

And Lescarbeault's new orb, quite small,
Which he in transit with his glass hath seen;
Nearest the orb of day, they "Vulcan" call,
Lost in the glories of the solar sheen;—

Complete the shining, wond'rous list
Of planets now to human science known;
Yet, doubtless, others still in space exist,
Whose light to this our orb hath never shone.

The milky way, that zone of suns;
The moon, meteors, constellations bright,
Perhaps a comet who his circuit runs,
Boreal and the Zodiacal light,—

With mysterious Nebula:
These are the gorgeous drapery of thy arch,
O splendid night,—fit counterpart of day,
Where wonders, crowd on wonders in their march.

Who can go forth at night, and gaze
On the fair moon, and constellated sky,
And not be lost in wonder, love, and praise,
To their great Author, God! our Friend on high?

ON A MONUMENTAL SLAB.

Reader hast thou a hope of heaven,
And dost thou know thy sins forgiven?
Stop, think a moment, and be wise,
Improve *this* moment as it flies.

A REGRET.

For having killed a beautiful butterfly for a young lady who was making a collection of insects.

How cruel! how cruel! it makes my heart bleed
To think how it struggled and seem'd to say " spare,"
But then for a moment my tenderness fled,
For its wings, and colors were pretty and fair.

Reluctant I pierc'd it, then turn'd from the sight,
I did it in haste, but sure never again
Will I torture a thing so pretty and bright,
For I feel in my breast keen anguish and pain.

If others can do it they may if they will,
But gold would not tempt me to do it again,
For years may roll on, I shall think of it still,
And think of it too with keen anguish and pain.

I did it, but Hannah, she made the request,
For her I was cruel, and kill'd the poor thing,
But she with myself felt a pain in the breast,
With tears of regret we bedew'd its bright wing.

GOD'S WILL.

The rill, which from the mountain leaps,
Bespeaks a God, and nature's laws;
The wind, which o'er the mountain sweeps,
Reminds us of the Great First Cause!
And every zephyr, every rill,
Bids us obey His sovereign will!

The lightning, darting from the sky,
The thunder, rolling in the cloud,
Alike proclaim a God on high!
And speak to hearts rebellious, proud,
In accents which with terror fill,
Commanding them to do His will.

The oceans, rolling in their might,
Wave, after wave to us declare,
In concert with yon orb of light,
His Being present everywhere;—
And as they nature's laws fulfil,
Bid us obey His sacred will!

The mountain, vale, and flowery plain,
The rock, the river, and the wood,
The snow, the hail, and fruitful rain,
Proclaim a Being wise and good;
They move the heart, so hard and chill,
To yield submission to His will!

The numerous tribes of living things,
That walk the land, or swim the sea;
That creep the earth, or soar on wings,
Their voices join in harmony.
Earth, air, and sea their praises fill—
Instinctively they do His will!

Shall man, the noblest of them all,
Made in their Author's image pure—
Made lord, to govern great and small,
With being ever to endure;
The masterpiece of matchless skill,
Shall he neglect to do His will?

Let demons rave in dark despair,
And send their curses to His throne!
Let mortals bow in humble prayer,
And own Him God, and God alone!
Then haste their steps to Zion's hill,
And learn, and do His holy will.

Soon, soon with angel choirs above,
The obedient child of earth shall sing,
In rapturous strains of melting love,
The praises of the Eternal King!
In notes seraphic, pure and shrill,
For all the wonders of His will!

But sinners who reject His grace,
And rise rebellious to His power,
Must all be banish'd from His face,
Beneath His wrath forever cower!
Their cup of anguish this shall fill,
That they despis'd their Maker's will!

ON A MOTHER AND HER CHILD'S STONE.

If rarest worth and beauty's bloom
Exempted mortals from the tomb,
We should not round this sacred spot
Mourn the sweet babe and mother's lot.

THE FLIES MY LITTLE PETS.

The little busy, active flies
Flew o'er my face, lit on my eyes,
And seem'd to say "Sluggard arise,"
   And I arose.

And then so joyful they appear'd,
Their music sweet my spirit cheer'd,
Less grateful I than they, I fear'd
   For night's repose.

Then when I kneel'd to offer prayer,
And thank and ask a Father's care,
They my devotions seem'd to share,
   And buzz'd amens.

And when I read the Sacred Book,
Well pleas'd they seem'd by act and look,
As legs and wings they briskly shook,
   My happy friends.

O may the faithful teaching fly,
Repeat the lesson if I lie
Too late, when I should up and try
   To do some good.

Like them be gentle, active too,
And fly about and duty do,
And every hour find something new
   For gratitude.

Dear playful, trusting, little things,
Forever on your legs or wings,
At home with peasant, princes, kings,
   Partial to none.

In cottage, palace, church and street,
My little friends I ever meet,
And always with a buzz they greet
   In sweetest tone.

Be careful now, MY LITTLE PETS;
For you the spider spreads his nets,
And naughty house-wives poison sets
   To kill you all.

But if you take my kind advice,
And open wide your little eyes,
Avoiding every false disguise,
   You'll live till Fall.

In winter you are seldom seen,
Endure you cannot air so keen,
But long to me the months between
   Your go and come.

But when the sun shall melt the snow,
And the warm wind shall gently blow,
Then my dear constant friends, I know,
      Will buzz and hum.

Then I a welcome will prepare,
Of honey, fruits, and dainties rare,
And kindly bid you all to share,
      And feel at ease.

Come not alone—bring all your friends,
Invite them each to bring their tens,
For to remain till summer ends,
      Then go or freeze.

God made all creatures, great and small,
For some good end, but since man's "Fall,"
Suffering and death includes them all,
      Exempted none.

Shall there no reparation be?
Yes, God is just, and we shall see
From bondage all His creatures free,
      Nor longer groan.

Then you, my pretty darling flies,
If I am good, in yonder skies
Shall meet, where pleasure never dies,
      Our God to see.

With powers enlarg'd to feel and know,
Things darkly seen while here below,
From whence, to whence, our spirits flow—
      Eternity.

But now I leave this pleasing theme,
And wake refresh'd from poet's dream,
Enlighten'd by a heavenly beam
      To be more wise.

Avoiding every sinful snare,
Discarding every anxious care,
Trusting in God, in humble prayer,
      To win the prize.

FORGIVENESS.

'Tis sweet to forgive when another hath err'd,
And when we have err'd, be forgiven;
A mystical healing is found in the word
"Forgive"—'tis the balsam of heaven.

While onward we move 'mid the evils of life,
'Tis often we need be forgiven;
Since 'tis human to err, where error is rife,
But forgiveness reminds us of heaven.

That man should be pitied who never forgives;
For God will not speak him forgiven.
In darkness and sorrow, unpardon'd he lives;
Unpardon'd, he misses of heaven!

O, may I show mercy when others offend,
And cheerfully speak them forgiven;
By this often a foe is chang'd to a friend,
And thus changing earth into heaven.

Who forgives not his brother, himself cannot know
The pleasure of pardon from Heaven,
And if mercy we ask, the same we must show,
And forgive or ne'er be forgiven.

Dear Father of mercy, Who loves me Thy child,
Once guilty, I now am forgiven;
I thank Thee for pardon, on me Thou hast smil'd,
I feel it—an earnest of heaven.

My bosom now swells with unspeakable praise,
My song is "Forgiven, forgiven;"
Precious words to my soul, and rhymes in my lays
So smoothly, and sweetly with heaven.

CONTENTMENT.

Contentment is the soul of ease,
Its absence is the soul of pain,
In vain we strive to bless or please—
The discontented will complain.

But if contentment fills the breast,
The common ills of life we bear
As mercies in disguises dress'd,
As blessings, though dark robes they wear.

The patient, humble, childlike soul,
Endures each momentary ill,
Knowing, when time shall cease its roll,
Peace, love, and joy their soul shall fill.

THE SLANDERER.

I pity sure the envious man,
Whose object ever is to plan,
To spoil another's honest fame;
Who ne'er can find a moment's rest,
If others by the world are blest,
Till he hath blasted their good name.

I pity him, I scorn him too,
Whose venom'd pen, and tongue would strew
Life's pathway with the thorns of hate;
Who knows, nor feels a moment's *bliss*,
Unless the fiendlike stab and kiss
That fever'd, hellish *bliss* create.

I pity him, his neighbor's bane,
Who proudly calls another vain,
Because another higher climbs,
Winning world-wide the meed of praise,
With words of love, in measured lays,
With swelling cadence, pleasing rhymes.

I pity him, but wish him far
Remov'd, no more man's bliss to mar;
No more to cast his deadly shade,
Upon the path where virtues shine,
And the bright rays of grace combine;
May he that path no more invade.

I pity him, and will forgive
His sin, and love him while I live,
If he a penitent will be:
And for the future, like a man,
With kindly feelings ever plan
To bless, not curse society.

TO MISS ELLEN MATHEWSON.

SYMPATHETICALLY ON THE SUDDEN DEATH OF HER MOTHER.

See we now by faith in glory
She who lived for Christ on earth,
Where she told the Gospel story,
To her children from their birth,
Lived her fourscore years and four—
Died to live for evermore.

Suddenly her Saviour call'd her
To enjoy her great reward,
With the blood-wash'd He installed her,
Ever there to praise Her Lord,
O, what rapture in her song,
Which shall last her being long.

Father, Mother reunited
In eternal bonds of love,
Parents, Children there delighted,
In that blissful clime above,
O may they who live be there,
Crowns of life with them to wear.

May we emulate her graces;
Useful live while here below,
Walk the path which duty traces,
Only Jesus love and know;
Win with her the heavenly prize—
Rest eternal in the skies.

O how blest are they who enter
To the presence of their Lord.
He of bliss the eternal centre,
Earth and heaven with one accord
Raise their pæans to His throne,
While He claims us as His own.

EARTH AND HEAVEN.

Winter born, and winter ended,
Are the changing years of earth;
Heaven's a spring and summer blended,
Knows no end, and knew no birth.

Fading flowers of rarest beauty
Strew our pathway to the tomb;
Heaven's unfading, angel's duty
Is to waft their sweet perfume.

Earth hath smiles, but soon in sadness
All her smiles are shrouded o'er;
Heaven's are lasting, all is gladness,
Pleasures ever, evermore.

Friendship, here a word oft spoken,
Oft a name without the thing;
But in heaven, the thing, and token
Angel poets ever sing.

Earth hath coined, and coffer'd treasures,
Pearls, and diamonds, costly prize;
Coins of love, and minted pleasures,
Is the treasure of the skies.

Earth hath honors, fame, and glory,
But how empty, trifling, vain;
List awhile, and hear the story
Of the conquering Christian's fame:

How when Christ in awful grandeur,
Comes the Judge of quick and dead;
Babe no more of Bethlehem's manger,
But a God! whose mighty tread

Shakes the pillars and foundations
Of His universe around;
Suns, and planets leave their stations
At His herald's trumpet sound!

Not an angel left to wonder,
Haste they all His train to swell;
Vivid lightnings, sevenfold thunder
Bursts the gloomy gates of hell!

Men forsake their dusty pillows;
Start to life in every clime,
From dark caves, and rolling billows;
While expires old hoary Time.

Men and devils stand before Him;
All confess He is the Lord,
Holy beings all adore Him,
Praise Him all in sweet accord.

Now He speaks, and every creature
Hears His voice with joy or dread;
Truth is mark'd on every feature,
Every subterfuge is fled!

Godlike honors, fame for ever;
Seated on the Conqueror's throne,
Glories which shall perish never,
Lot of those He calls "His own."

Such is heaven, and all who enter,
Jesus welcomes to His arms,
He, of bliss the eternal centre,
Now exhibits all His charms!

While on earth my footsteps wander,
May I live for heaven above;
On its glories ever ponder,
Love my God, my Jesus love.

PATIENCE.

Patience, is a lovely flower,
Blooming constant all the year,
Brighest in the darkest hour,
Green, when all beside is sere.

Sweetens pain and sorrow's cup,
Mingles pleasure with our care,
Lifts the fainting spirits up,
Spreads contentment everywhere.

Sweet contentment, patience, hope,
Sisters smiling, always fair,
Us they cheer, and to us ope
Future pleasures, bright, and rare.

O, how sad our earth would be,
Banish'd were they from our sphere,
Not a spot where we could flee
Aught to find, to bless and cheer.

Patience, be my constant friend;
Then contented shall I smile,
Hoping always to the end,
Cheerful, grateful, all the while

TO A CO-LABORER IN THE GOSPEL VINEYARD, Dr. J. P.,

WHOSE DUTIES CALLED HIM AWAY FROM HOME AND FAMILY FOR A SEASON.

Toil on, toil on, through life's short day,
And cultivate Emmanuel's land,
To sinners preach, for sinners pray,
And give to all the friendly hand;
Hoping that all may turn and live—
That all to God their hearts may give.

Arduous thy duty, full of care,
But Christ is with thee in thy toil;
He'll listen to thy fervent prayer,
And grant thee strength thy foes to spoil;
He'll light thy pathway to the skies,
And crown thee with the Gospel prize.

Go, and thy mission fully prove,
Go, rouse the sleeping, call, "To arms,"
Bid Zion's hosts in concert move,
Point them to crowns, and conquering palms,
And say, "Be firm, be bold, be strong,
Though fierce the conflict, 'tis not long."

Beware of earth's alluring snares,
Its pleasures, honors, and its gold ;
They are the source of constant cares,
And for them Christ hath oft been sold,
But could you all the world control,
What profit if you lose the soul ?

Soon will the toilsome day be o'er,
And thy last battle shall be won,
Then with the fathers gone before,
You'll join to praise the Three-in-One,
For all the wonders of the grace,
By which you ran the Christian race.

Does duty call thee now away
From fireside sweets to roam afar ?
There, in the clime of endless day,
Your crown shall shine with many a star
Which you shall win to Christ your Lord,
While thus you strain the social cord.

WRITTEN AFTER A SHOWER—
WEEP NOT FLOWERS.

Weep not flowers: all is gladness,
Nature smiles, free from sadness,
Birds are singing merrily;
Lambs are frisking o'er the lea,
Fish are sporting in the sea,
All is life and full of glee—
        Weep not.

Weep not flowers: in thy beauty
Bloom and smile, 'tis thy duty;
Cheerful nature speaks to thee,
All I hear, and all I see,
Language full of ecstasy,
Sure to you, if not to me—
        Weep not.

Wept my Saviour! weep I may
Tears repentant every day;
He for sinners, I for sin,
Till my heart is pure within;
His the tears to set us free,
From our guilt and misery;
To Him mortals bend the knee
In faith, hope and charity;
Weep, then smile, for these remain,
Peace and joy are in their train.

TEDIOUS, TEDIOUS.

COMPOSED WHEN RECOVERING FROM A LONG AND DANGEROUS ILLNESS, AND WRITTEN BY MY PHYSICIAN AS I DICTATED.

Tedious, tedious, O how tedious
Are the restless hours of pain;
Fever'd blood and throbbing temples,
Faltering lungs and aching brain.

Long and gloomy is the night-watch,
Long and sad the watch of day,
Linger they—sure, hoary Time
Hath grown weary on his way.

Gentle noise of mouse, or cricket
Sounds a riot to the ear,
Closing blind, or shutting wicket,
Earth, and air-quake both appear.

Buzzing fly seems quite a tempest,
Ticking clock like thunder peals,
When it strikes, then all creation
Rattles, rumbles, rocks and reels.

Carriage o'er the mountain pavement
Sounds a crash, a wreck of worlds,
Such is man's disorder'd sense,
When his brain with fever whirls.

Seething hot my bed and pillow,
Turn I, but no ease I find,
Restless as the ocean's billow,
Death, though cruel, would be kind.

Faint I now in infant weakness,
Fades the scenes of earth away;
All is dark! O, what a darkness;
Will there come another day?

Gentle whispers, heartfelt sighing,
Rouse me to my sense again;
Is it so? ah! am I dying,
Fatal archer, am I slain?

Now my lips the cordial moistens,
Down my throat it trickles life,
Sure it is life's pure elixir,
From the hand of that dear wife.

Now I rest, and quiet slumbers
All medicinal are mine,
Now the morn awakes my vision;
Glorious sun, I see thee shine.

Day and night I'm convalescing,
Scenes of life before me rise;
O, may Heaven, with aid supernal,
Guide me ever to the skies.

A THOUGHT.

Vesuvius from her crater throws
Her burning lava o'er the plains,
So from the " still " fire liquid flows,
To fill with death the drunkard's veins.

It flows through every street and lane,
And spreads destruction in its way;
The source of sorrow, anguish, pain,
The bane of night, the curse of day.

THE MISSION OF PAIN.

"For He doth not afflict willingly nor grieve the children of men."—Lam. iii. 33.

My heart is sear'd with pain,
And doth the good God this?
My feeble strength doth wane,
I know no earthly bliss.

Father divine, I know,
Grieveth me not in wrath,
Though heavily dealt the blow,
Yet love His purpose hath.

Th' enticing joys of earth
To earth contract the sight,
But joys of heavenly birth
Ask broader higher light.

In summer's noon of day,
The world in beauty beams,
Trees, fields, and wat'ry way,
In flood of glory gleams.

Would we have view more wide,
Systems on systems see,
Orbs in their orbits glide
Unto infinity;

Then evening's shade must fall,
And high noon's glory fade,
That darkness' heavy pall,
May show what light hath hid.

Afflictions to the mind
Reveal the things of God,
We walk by faith, and find
Rich mercies in the rod.

PETER'S FALL.

From Jesus I so far did stray,
I ceas'd to watch, I ceas'd to pray;
Temptation came, Him I denied—
"I know Him not," in wrath I cried.
Thrice was accus'd, as oft replied
"I know Him not," in scorn, and pride,
The cock's shrill note my conscience stung,
My soul in bitter anguish wrung.
A look from Jesus heal'd my wound,
A Saviour then indeed I found;
Those bitter tears He wiped away,
To Heaven I rais'd a grateful lay.

How many, Peter like, can say
"I've ceas'd to watch, I've ceas'd to pray;"
And have like him their Lord denied,
Indulging unbelief and pride?—
Not thrice alone, but oft each day,
Till weeks, months, years have roll'd away—
Who yet may turn by faith, and see
Jesus Who wept for you and me;
Whose tears of pity for our woe
Shall cause repentant tears to flow;
Whose smile those bitter tears shall stay,
And prompt to heaven a grateful lay.

A FAITHFUL FRIEND.

Is there on earth this treasure found,
A friend that's faithful, kind, and true;
Who, when we've blam'd, they feel the wound,
Blame us in love when blame is due?

If sure a treasure rare as this
Is found on earth, O tell me where,
That I may feel the sacred bliss,
The smile of such a friend to share.

But earth hath not that treasure now,
Let Calvary tell the reason why;
Yet they who to our Jesus bow,
This friend may find above the sky.

There,
For ever and ever,
Where pain enters never,
And death cannot sever,
Thy sister and brother now reigns,
That friendship to share,
Be constant in watching and fervent in prayer,
Then Mary Ann too, at last shall be there,
Where death cannot sever,
And pain enters never,
For ever and ever,
With Jesus to reign,
And sing hallelujah, amen and
Amen.

THE BIBLE.

O precious book, so full of truth,
A light and guide to age and youth,
A book of more intrinsic worth
Then all the gems and gold of earth.

On every page new beauties shine,
Brilliant the thought, the theme sublime,
Here flows the purest streams of love,
From God the fountain-head above.

I was born June twenty-two, eighteen hundred four,
And have read the whole Bible seven times and threescore,
And expect if I live to another birthday,
"I have read it again" to be able to say.
When but twelve, to my dear father now in glory,
I had read every word of the Old Old Story,
Once in four days I read it, and once in thirteen,
Having nights of sweet sleep the long readings between.
In the year sixty-six with an object in view,
The dear, precious volume, I read thirteen times through,
If there is one living—will that one please report,
Who has read it as often, and in times as short?
The numbers are millions I indulge not a doubt,
Who may never have read the blest Bible throughout,
Yet have lived meek, and holy, a pattern to all,
While I through temptations have oft suffered a fall.
But, thanks to God's mercy, I still read with delight
Its truths every morning, oft at noon, and at night,
Prize, dear READER, this Book of God's revelation,
And learn the great Science of human Salvation.

THE CEDAR AND THE WILLOW GLOOM.

Composed when the cholera was taking away hundreds around me, and myself suffering with an attack of it.

The Cedar and the Willow gloom,
(Where dust of friends in peace is laid;)
I ever hop'd that there my tomb,
Would be beneath their sacred shade,
But far from home I now must die—
With strangers here my dust must lie.

No kindred's tear o'er me is shed,
No wife or child these eyes shall close,
A stranger friend beside my bed,
A stranger's want of pity shows;
Yet kind enough to drop a tear,
But not like those of kindred dear.

I love the spot where life began,
Where infancy to manhood grew,
Where ever varying currents ran
Of hopes the many, fears the few;
But far away in space and time—
No more for me that genial clime.

I will not murmur or complain,
For a kind Father plac'd me here;
And here I willingly remain,
For He's a Father lov'd and dear.
Too wise to err, I'll love Him still,
And bow submissive to His will.

Yet lingers round my memory scenes
Of days and years of pleasures fled,
The hill, the wood, and sloping green,
The churchyard with its slumbering dead;
The Cedar and the Willow gloom,
I would have chosen for my tomb.

"WHEN SHALL I COME AND APPEAR BEFORE GOD?"

O, when shall I come and appear before God,
To bow in His presence, submit to His rod,
And hope for His pardon, and look for His grace,
And feel that His presence makes sacred the place?
I long for Thy courts—to dwell in Thy sight,
The darkness of nature illum'd by Thy light,
My heart tuned to praise for His mercy divine,
And by faith claim the Godhead as sacredly mine.
O! Jesus, my Saviour, I come to Thy throne,
No plea but Thy merits—Thy merits alone;
Sufficient Thy blood every stain to remove,
And fill my whole soul with the fulness of love.
I pant for Thy courts as the hart for the brook,
With sorrow, I mourn that I ever forsook
Thy gates, O loved Zion—Thy altars of prayer,
And covered my soul with the shroud of despair.
No more will I wander; but, close to Thy side,
Securely I'll rest—in Thy Word will confide,
'Till the summons shall come to call me away
From the darkness of earth to the region of day.

Sunnyside, July 1870.

I WOULD NOT DIE.

I would not die: I wish to live,
And to the world my talent give
Which God to me hath given,
A little good on earth to do;
And when my pilgrimage is through,
To find a home in heaven.

I'd live, to tell the young beware
Of every sinful, subtle snare
Spread in their morning way;
To show life's noontide dangers too,
And point them to the pathway true,
Leading to endless day.

I'd live, to council age mature,
And ever urge them to secure
A treasure in the skies;
By my example, show the road
That leads unerringly to God,
Where pleasure never dies.

I'd live, because my life hath been
A checker'd scene of doubt and sin;
But now I would be wise,
And show to all, both foe, and friend,
How well by grace a life may end,
And, conquering, win the prize.

I'd live, my God to glorify,
I'd live, that I may never die
The death of endless shame;
But in the courts of bliss and joy,
Eternally my powers employ
To praise God's sacred name.

I'd rather die than live one day
In sinful pleasures' path to stray,
Away from Christ, my all;
Yes, while I write, let welcome death
Marble my frame, and stop my breath,
Rather than live to fall.

I've lived to see my century's noon,
And still enjoy the sacred boon—
The gift of pardoning love;
My noon of life hath long since sped,
The evening shades around me spread,
But all is bright above.

GOD EVER NEAR.

How mighty, wise, and ever nigh
The God, on Whom my hopes rely!
No danger will I ever fear,
For He, Omnipotent, is near;
In darkness, as in shining day,
My sure defence, my constant stay.
If fiendlike hosts my soul assail,
I will not fear—they can't prevail;
His promise sure—" That as my day
My strength shall be," while in the way
Of duty, I my course pursue,
With Jesus ever in my view,
As safe, as though my course were run,
And listening to the words, " Well done,
Thou good and faithful servant," take
The crown of life for My own sake.
Bold and courageous, I will stand
And fight in our Emmanuel's band,
Till all opposing foes are slain,
Then victor with my Chieftain reign.

SNUG LITTLE FIRE.

How pleasing to sit, on a cold wintry night,
In a room which is heated with anthracite coal;
How gently it burns with its cherry red light,
While the blue gaseous flames upward lazily roll.

I sit and remember the days of my youth,
At the foot of Manadnoch with grandparents dear;
Where I liv'd—yes, I liv'd—an emphatic truth,
Through spring, summer, autumn and the rest of the year.

The winter 'twas drear, but the old folks were kind,
And a "holiday" sure were those evenings so long;
We had comforts, and food, for body and mind,
Such as nuts, apples, cider, the book and the song.

But the fire—yes, the fire—how shall I describe
Such a forest of fuel, and mountain of flame?
Enough to have warm'd a large Indian tribe,
Or Napoleon's host when from Moscow he came.

Around it in circle at distance we sit,
All amus'd with its snapping, its crackle and roar;
My aunts (blessed souls) they had stockings to knit,
While my uncles were whittling all over the floor.

Snug under the table, old Towzer he snor'd,
And snug in the corner our old Tabby did purr;
No clatter of windows though the tempest roar'd,
For grandsire had so fix'd them that nothing could stir.

How blest were those moments, and 'tis with delight
That I think of their pleasures though long years have
    fled;
No cares, and no sorrows, my young heart did blight,
Not a foe for to fear, not a danger to dread.

Since those blessed days many sorrows I've known;
Through much tribulation I have wander'd in woe;
Kind friends at a distance, while I, all alone,
In anguish have suffer'd what no mortal can know.

My grandparents dear, ah! they sleep in the dust,
My aunts, and my uncles, have gone down to the grave,
My pastor, dear Payson, is now with the just,
With the most of his flock whom he labor'd to save.

My playmates are scatter'd o'er all the wide earth;
But ah! some now moulder in a premature tomb
By rum, the destroyer; while others, whose worth
Show the fruits of the Spirit from faith's sacred bloom.

But those blessed days cannot ever return,
Yet the present are blest, for our God is the same,
If we childlike submit of Jesus to learn,
We both now, and for ever, may happiness claim.

Let earth have its changes, and men their desire,
Let the conqueror boast, o'er his conquered foes,
I'll sit down content, by my "SNUG LITTLE FIRE,"
And on Christ, my Redeemer, will calmly repose.

JESUS IS MINE.

Jesus is mine, my soul with rapture cries;
And I am His, by sacred, heavenly ties.
Nothing on earth, beside Him, I desire;
To sing, His praise, my lips shall never tire.
Jesus is mine, O what a wondrous thought,
And I am His, He hath my ransom bought—
Not with the price of rubies, pearls, or gold,
Nor all the wealth which worlds, on worlds, unfold—
But with His precious blood, more priceless far
Then earth, sun, moon, and every beaming star.
Jesus is mine, O can it,—can it be,—
That I, once vile, and distant far from Thee,
Can call my own, as Saviour, Brother, Friend,
Thee, Jesus, Thee, Whose love shall never end?
Yes, He is mine, let all within me raise
To Him, the song of sweet adoring praise.
Yes, He is mine, and let the tale be told,
He found me near where flaming billows roll'd;
Where hope's last ray, shed but a flickering light
On the dark shroud, of night—eternal night,
Whose mists were gathering fast, with awful gloom,
Around my soul, to seal its fearful doom!

He found me there—another step, and oh!
My soul had plung'd in dark, unfathomed woe!
There, there He found—and found me but to save.
He snatch'd me thence, as from the burning wave.
O precious Jesus! wondrous grace divine!
He snatch'd me thence, and bid me call Him mine.
Mine, mine Thou art! and mine shall ever be,
And I am Thine to all eternity!

IS HE MINE.

Is He mine—O what a treasure,
Is He mine—O what a bliss,
Is He mine—O what a pleasure,
Surely, earth hath naught like this;
 Yes, I claim Him, as my own,
 He, His love to me hath shown.

Is He your's—then give Him glory,
Is He your's—a Saviour near,
Is He your's—then tell the story
Of His precious love so dear.
 Claim Him, claim Him, as your own,
 He, His love to you hath shown.

Greater love hath no man ever
Shown than this, his life to give
For a friend,—but never, never
Died he that a foe might live;
    But for foes, like you and me,
    Jesus died on Calvary.

Precious Saviour, don't reject Him,
He is your's; by faith you may—
Now, this moment—now expect Him,
All your sins to take away;
    Claim Him, claim Him, as your own,
    He, His love to all hath shown.

Haste while Jesus bids you enter
At the door He's opened wide,
Cast your all on Him, and venture
All, and in His word confide;
    He will claim you as His own;
    O, what love to us is shown.

PURE COLD WATER.

Wine and brandy, never, never,
Pure cold water, ever, ever;
Yes, drink the healthful water cup,
Whene'er you breakfast, dine, or sup.

Wine and brandy—want and sorrow,
Pain to-day and death to-morrow;
Wine and brandy—fighting, lying,
Wife and children sobbing, sighing.

Pure cold water—health and treasure,
Peaceful conscience, lasting pleasure;
Pure cold water—kind and cheerful,
Wife and children never fearful.

ON MY ONLY SON'S TOMBSTONE.

The cherub host rejoic'd anew
When this dear child bid earth adieu;
Too lovely here with us to stay,
They bore him to the realms of day.

NEW AND OLD YEAR—1870-71.

O, what a lovely world is ours,
Blest with sunshine, wind, and showers;
Clad in green or robes of white,
Blest with seasons, day and night,
Flowers, and fruits, in time appear,
To crown for us the smiling year.

But our years how soon they fly,
Flowers, and fruits, they fade and die,
Death's chill winter with its blasts,
O'er loveliest scenes its mantle casts;
But faith, and hope, our spirits cheer,
With prospects of a brighter year.

That brighter year is ours at last,
Eighteen hundred seventy's past,
And eighteen hundred seventy-one,
Greets us with its shining sun;
May we with joy without a tear,
Spend this our own new happy year.

May sons of earth learn war no more,
May peace reign from shore to shore,
May every virtue, every grace,
Be practis'd by the human race;
All bid adieu to doubt and fear,
And all enjoy a happy year.

Could sin be banish'd from our sphere,
And usher in that glorious year,
By sacred prophets long foretold,
Superior to the age of gold,
Then Gospel Eden would appear,
And Jesus reign throughout the year.

BIRTHDAY.

Written on my birthday, June 22nd, 1869.

Another year of life hath fled,
And fleeing I remain,
While many of my friends are dead,
I live in hope and pain;
When will my hour of rescue come,
And I, with them, find heaven my home?

Three scores and five my years of woe,
But soon must come my last,
Perhaps this year will lay me low,
My sands are running fast;
But if another year I live,
May I, to God its moments give.

I feel and know He is my Friend,
O may I ever feel
His friendship not with life to end,
Infinity its seal;
Through all eternity His love,
To be my bliss with saints above.

A POEM,

On the Picnic, of the Three Sabbath Schools, of the Great St. James Street Wesleyan Methodist Church, held September 12th, 1871. Read at the Young Men's Association of said Church.

Who, who of our number will not gratefully smile,
To think of our Picnic in the grove at Belœil?

'Twas a lovely day on the twelfth of September,
One in life's history we delight to remember,
How cheerful the morn, how clear and bright the sun shin'd
To favor us—all nature its beauties combin'd.

At the station we met quite a host young and old,
Sight truly amusing for the eye to behold;
After a few moments of quite pleasing delay
We all took our seats, then mov'd quickly away
Under bridge, over streets, around curves we rattle,
The children amus'd keeping up a brisk prattle,
Till we came to the bridge which spans the broad river,
And then when they spoke we could hear a slight quiver,
For as sudden as thought their bright day chang'd to night.
No wonder they shudder'd, as a quick flash of light

Darted into their eyes—then all darkness again,
The sudden transition giving optical pain;
But the darkness soon ended, and then the bright day
Dispell'd every fear, and we all darted away
Through fields of bright verdure, and by groves of young
    trees,
Seeing things distant, and near, which all of us please.

God was answering our prayers—in giving delight
To all the dear children—they were happy and bright,
And sang the sweet tunes they had learn'd at the schools,
In praise to Him, Who in love, the universe rules.

But now rises before us the mount of Belœil,
We see in each countenance awaken'd a smile,
But the smiles were chang'd in a moment to sadness,
To smile near that bridge would be token of madness,
Where a few years ago near a hundred were slain,
German passengers on board an emigrant train!
As we pass the sad spot we with gratitude raise
Thanks to God, our Protector, Who guards all our ways.

A few minutes more, then our rail journey ended,
And soon to the grove, walk or ride we ascended,
And astonishingly soon we spread through the wood,
A fine scene for an artist—while eating our food,
Amusing, and grotesque, was the view all around,
Instead of tables, and chairs, we us'd the dry ground.

Some ate scarcely thinking of milk, coffee or tea;
Not so the gentleman who provided for me,
His shining tea kettle, and his alcohol fire,
Gave a fine cup of tea—none could better desire.

'Twas pleasing to see the "Howard" of our city,
His fire burning, kettle boiling, showing pity
To all who needed, or wish'd for a cup
Of the beverage, which old, and young like to sup.

After doing full justice to cakes, tarts and pies,
We all took the course which seem'd best in our eyes.
We talk'd of the "Children" as we came by the way,
Who now were the "Children" 'twas a puzzle to say,
For old men, and maidens, did with each other vie,
And young men, and matrons, to excel seem'd to try,
In the sports of the hour, which were healthful and pure,
Which "Fossils" would object to alone is quite sure.

Some in running, and jumping, and swinging, excell'd,
Some in choosing their partners, or in being repell'd,
Some in flying the kite, or in bending the bow
Were experts—some in climbing the trees made a show;
The boys (if such a term is admissible here,
Where the men are all boys) in their sack races were
    queer.

Though the eldest perhaps in the midst of the scene,
I felt rejuvinated—not more than sixteen!
Some climb'd the rough mount, for a panoramic view
Of St. Lawrence, Champlain, and the winding Richelieu,
Of villages, towns, and the proud city their home,
Then footsore, and halting, to the "grove" back they come.

But the scene most amusing, and pleasing to all,
Was the "Children's gathering," at our dear Pastor's call,
By scores, and by hundreds in close circles around,
Thick as bees when they swarm—they quite cover the ground;
Then they all sang "A Grace," with a thankful good will,
And of choice cakes, and apples, they each took their fill;
Then sang about Jesus—melodious the song,
Did angels in chorus, hover over the throng,
And far off in the skies, the sweet anthem prolong?

But time flies, O how swiftly, the hour it is come,
We must leave the green grove, for our far distant home;
The cars are in waiting, we soon enter, and wait
For a season, to be sure that all things were "straight;"
Our fine steam horse is snorting, impatient his stay,
The word being given, he darts quickly, away,
Over the once fatal bridge in safety we move,
Then fly rapidly homeward on rails, firm, and smooth.

The morning it was pleasant, the noon calm and bright,
As pleasant, and calm, were the approaches of night:
The sun set in glory, when his day's work was done:
May we all take a lesson from the beautiful sun,
In our orbits of duty with constancy run,
A blessing to all—as in his beams all are blest,
Then departing in triumph, go home to our "rest."

Through the world-wide wonder we rumbled and roll'd,
" Victoria bridge," a work stupendous and bold,
And here as we pass all is shrouded in gloom,
Reminding us of the way from life, to the tomb;
But the city beyond hath no feature of heaven,
Except in God's children whose sins are forgiven.

Our little folks, though tired, were contented;—and calm
As the evening enjoy'd—whose breath was all balm.
Quite slowly we mov'd from the bridge to the station,
Where safely ended our Picnic Celebration.
Now with kindly " good nights " to our homes we repair,
To close the blest day with thanksgivings, and prayer.

Who, who of our number, does not gratefully smile
To think of our Picnic in the " grove " at Belœil?

G

AN ADIEU TO MY COUNTRY.*

> " Breathes there a man with soul so dead,
> Who never to himself hath said
> This is my own my native land?
> Whose heart hath ne'er within him burn'd,
> As home his footsteps he hath turn'd
> From wandering on a foreign strand?
> If such there be, go mark him well,
> For him no minstrel strain shall swell.
> High though his titles, proud his name,
> Boundless his wealth as wish can claim;
> Despite his titles, power and pelf,
> The wretch concentred all in self,
> Living shall forfeit fair renown,
> And doubly dying, shall go down
> To the vile earth from whence he sprung,
> Unwept, unhonored, and unsung."—Sir W. Scott.

When I think of my country so noble and free,
My breast heaves with anguish, it is no more for me;
At distance I wander ne'er again to enjoy
The home of my childhood, where, a privileg'd boy,
I roam'd at my pleasure, 'mid its scenes of delight,
Nor dream'd I, that ever, they should fade from my sight.

* Composed on the cars between Albany and Montreal, May 26th, 1841.

My country, I love thee !—thy green hills and thy dales,
Thy fields of sweet beauty, thy rich meadows and vales,
Thy smooth flowing rivers, and thy brooklets so pure,
Thy forests of grandeur may they ever endure.
Thy flourishing towns of manufactures and trade,
Thy broad acres disturb'd by the plough or the spade,
Thy vast regions for grazing, where cattle now roam,
And thy vaster wide prairies, the buffalo's home;
Thy rivers and cataracts how truly sublime,
For beauty and grandeur excell'd in no clime,
Thy long range of mountains capp'd with ice and with snow,
Birthplace of deep rivers, source of wealth as they flow;
Thy vessels of commerce, and iron ships of war,
Floating thy star-blazon'd flag which despots abhor;
May it float in its pride on lake, ocean, and sea,
Till oppression shall cease, and all nations are free !
Thy mines of treasure, an inexhaustible store,
Lead, iron, silver, copper, either pure or in ore,
Quicksilver, coal, zinc, and many others untold,
And last, but not least, thy pure platinum and gold.

The arch of the continent thy railroads now span,
Bespeaking the all conquering genius of man,
Thy telegraph's flash over land—under ocean,
To check, or to aid, the world's great commotion,
This lightning express, the nerve of peace, war and trade,
By it treaties, and fortunes, are broken or made.

Thy common school system so extensive and free,
Where the black, red and white, rich and poor, without fee,
May study all science, and may such knowledge obtain
As is needful for all—and assist all to gain
Positions in life, which our Great Author design'd
Every intelligent human being should find.
Thy courts of strict justice so impartial to all,
Thy writ Habeas Corpus takes the body at call,
Thy trial by jury with challenge appended,
And prisoners by counsel may each be defended.

Thy churches where the truths of the gospel are taught,
No compulsion, each claiming the freedom of thought,
The Bible, plain guide book, throughout life to the skies,
A free open Bible none too highly can prize,
Free Schools, free Church, free Bible, thy bulwark shall stand,
And America ever be God's chosen land.

No despot, no autocrat, no tyrant to sway
The iron sceptre o'er slaves who bow, cringe and obey,
But democracy pure where the "Ballot Box" reigns;
And broken forever is the proud tyrant's chains.
May the God of all power make and keep you all pure,
Then thy free Institutions shall ever endure;
Thy noble Republic an example shall be,
And the lands now in bondage soon, soon shall be free.

FAREWELL TO MY COUNTRY, A LONG PAINFUL ADIEU!
I sink in deep sorrow as I take my last view
Of the home of my childhood, the land of my birth,
None like thee, – my dear country, on all the green earth.

My choice next to thee is where Victoria reigns,
A model of Queens, whose robe of state hath no stains,
God bless Her, and Her empire, with plenty and peace,
May the Lion, and the Eagle, from war ever cease,
The world's destiny We, if united, command,
May God grant Us union for an object so grand.

Old England, New England I now hail with pride,
In my heart both united where'er I reside,
And whene'er to the bosom of earth I return,
May one, or the other, of my dust be the urn!

TO HIS ROYAL HIGHNESS, PRINCE ARTHUR.

Permit, kind Sir, an aged Bard—
Who, battling with the world, is scarr'd
   From heel to crown!
But still is doing battle fair
With hosts of ills—pain, want and care,
   And envy's frown,—
      To present to You the following lines:—

The Poet's hand to You I gave,*
Not as a menial, or a slave,
But as a Son of Freedom's land,
Whose Sovereign people firmly stand
And say, "Who shall, or shall not be
The Ruler of Their country free."

Proud of my Country! well I may
Be proud,—and bless th' auspicious day
When the great Lincoln did proclaim,
Throughout Our vast slave-curs'd domain,

---

* I had been introduced to Him the day I composed this poem.

Freedom to all,—for all were bound
While slavery in Our Land was found;
Byword and scoff of every throne,
Where slaves in chains had ceased to groan.

Now Mother England owns with pride
Her Child, and lays Her sword aside,
And smiles to see Her Daughter fair
The robe of Sacred Justice wear.
A righteous Crown, and Sceptre too,
Of Truth to govern, not subdue.

Proud of Our Mother,—yes, 'tis truth—
Though stubborn in Our wayward Youth,
We hail with pride Her mighty power,
Which to a world will never cower—
Through all Our Land the good and wise
Her needed friendships highly prize—
The world in arms might strive in vain,
If We Her conquering power obtain,
To overthrow, or subjugate
Our Youthful, yet Our Manlike State.

Proud of Old England! yes, We will
Be proud, and pay Her homage still,
As Child to Parent only can
When Childhood ripens into Man!

We love Her Sovereign—Noble Queen,
Whose like the world has never seen;
Long may She live, and brighter shine
As She approaches life's decline ;
And when Her glorious course is run,
Reign by example in Her Son.

To Thee, Prince Arthur, young and fair,
Son of the most illustrious "Pair"
Which history's page to us reveals—
A truth the world admits and feels!
May you, Their virtues, emulate,
And rule in Hearts, if not in State!

This young Dominion, with delight
Claims You, as Her's, by sacred right!
Within Her border domiciled,
She claims Thee as Dominion's Child,
And pays to Thee the homage due,
Next to the Queen and Albert True!

May sacred pleasures long be Yours,
And bliss—which PIETY secures.
And here the Bard his song will end,
Your humble servant, Virtue's friend!

BARD OF NIAGARA.

31 Prince Street, Montreal, P. Q., D. C.

COPY

Of HIS ROYAL HIGHNESS, PRINCE ARTHUR's letter, sent to me under His Royal Seal, as an acknowledgment of the preceding poem :—

ROSE MOUNT, MONTREAL,
Nov. 25, 1869.

COLONEL ELPHINSTONE is desired by HIS ROYAL HIGHNESS PRINCE ARTHUR to acknowledge the receipt of the BARD OF NIAGARA's letter, forwarding two copies of some verses dedicated to the Prince.

HIS ROYAL HIGHNESS is much pleased with the loyal feelings displayed by the AUTHOR, as well as by the judicious and delicate manner in which he has given expression to those feelings.

HIS ROYAL HIGHNESS intends to keep the copy of these verses, as a reminiscence of his very agreeable visit to Canada.

BARD OF NIAGARA,
31 Prince Street, Montreal.

IN MEMORIAM.

BY A SYMPATHISING FRIEND.

The following consolatory lines were dedicated to Captain R. GARDNER, jun., on the death of his youthful and beloved wife, EMMA which occurred on the 25th January, 1870.

> The youthful loving friend so dear,
> Hath passed away from dreary earth;
> Affection sheds the bitter tear
> O'er loveliness and moral worth;
> But Faith, and Hope, those tears shall dry,
> For EMMA lives with Christ on high.
>
> Parents they weep, and Husband too,
> And all the circle of her friends,
> With tender love sincere and true;
> But He, the Husband, lowly bends,
> And feels the pangs of sacred grief.
> But Faith, and Hope, give sure relief.
>
> The reign of Winter yields its sway
> To Spring, and brighter Summer's hour;
> So death, on the great Quick'ning Day,
> Shall yield to our Redeemer's power,
> While Faith, and Hope, yield present bliss,
> Submissively the rod we kiss.

Yes, Faith, and Hope, point to the throne
Where sainted Emma joins to sing
The song in heaven's melodious tone,
With all the blest, to heaven's great King;
This thought dries up our every tear,
And makes our Jesus still more dear.

Soon, if like her we faithful be
To grace, our heavenly Father gives,
We'll join that holy company
Where Emma with her Saviour lives;
Where Faith is lost in the full view
Of Jesus, and the Father too.

O heavenly gift, Faith, Hope, and Love
Without them dark this earth would be;
Come, Holy Spirit, heavenly Dove
And fill us with the Sacred Three;
That all our hearts, consol'd, may tell
Our Master hath done all things well.

Then let us all the Saviour praise,
And humbly at His footstool bow;
Acknowledge Him in all our ways,
And claim His every promise now.
With Faith, Hope, Love, and every grace,
Secure with her in heaven a place.

FAITH—HOPE—LOVE.

" Faith, hope, charity, these three; and the greatest of these is charity."

Faith is the soul's far-seeing eye;
   It looks through all the plan of grace.
From Justice' sword uplifted high,
   To bleeding Mercy's suffering face!

Faith is the chain that reaches where
   The anchor, hope, in heaven is laid;
Not all the billows of despair,
   Thus moor'd can make the soul afraid.

Faith is the Christian's blazon'd shield,
   Inwrought with more than angel's skill;
Whose burnish'd front can never yield
   To all the fiery darts of ill.

Faith is the substance of the things
   That hope embraces in its view;
Borne on its strong, and soaring wings,
   The soul foretastes those pleasures true.

Faith is the telegraphic wire
  By which *Jehovah*, from his throne!
Conducts to earth the holy fire,
  Making HIS sovereign counsels known.*

In answer to the Christian's prayer,
  Around the globe, from pole to pole,
The sacred helix, truth shall bear
  To every dark, benighted soul!

"Faith moves the ARM that moves the worlds,"
  And when but as the mustard seed,
The mountain from its base it hurls,
  And breaks the earth's diurnal speed!†

Faith is the grace that leads the train:—
  Sinner, with humble heart believe.
You cannot trust *God's Word* in vain,
  Or doubt, and not HIS frown receive!

HOPE.

Hope is a star to guide and cheer
  The pilgrim on his weary way,
Its light forbids each rising fear,
  And peace, and joy, blend in its ray.

* Heb. xi. 3.   † Joshua x. 12, 13.

Hope is a tower on yonder plain,
   Beyond the dark domain of death!
The trav'ler sees the shining fane,
   And pants to breathe immortal breath.

Hope is an anchor to the soul,
   Entering within the sacred vail!
The winds may rise, the billows roll,
   Yet all is safe—it cannot fail!

Hope is the pathway to the skies,
   The shining track which prophets trod;
The peaceful road where all the wise
   Are journeying homeward to their GOD!

Hope is the medicine of life,
   A balm for every human ill.
She calms the passions, quells their strife
   With healing whispers, "Peace, be still."

Hope is a flower of sweet perfume.
   A plant exotic—from the skies;
It sheds its fragrance o'er the tomb,
   But in its native clime it dies!

If 'tis a star of brilliant ray;
   A beacon tower; an anchor sure;
A fragrant plant; a peaceful way;
   A medicine, the soul to cure;—

Why do not all the boon receive,
   And break the bondage of despair?
Renounce their sins, on CHRIST believe,
   And learn HIS easy yoke to bear?

LOVE.

Love is the atmosphere of heaven,
   Where spirits breathe eternal praise;
And all who know their sins forgiven
   With zephyrs thence their pæans raise.

Love is the magnet of the skies,
   Attracting every kindred part;
If low as earth the treasure lies,
   Some humble, contrite, sinner's heart—

Trembling, at once it heavenward tends,
   And, when from every hindrance freed,
Upward its willing course it bends,
   And flies to heaven with angel's speed.

Love, with its gravitating power,
   Draws heart to heart in union sweet;
And soon will come the happy hour,
   When Christians all, as one, shall meet:

As one, shall stand in firm array,
   The powers of darkness to oppose,
And usher in that glorious day,
   When Christ shall triumph o'er His foes!

Love is the greatest of the three,
   For 'twas when Faith and Hope were not;
And when they cease, it still will be
   The soul's unchanging, blissful lot.

'Tis the fulfilling of the law
   Which Faith, and Hope, could not fulfil;
Justice no more, His sword, shall draw,
   For Love obeys the Sovereign will.

Love is of God, and God is Love;
   And he that dwelleth in this grace
Dwelleth in God, as saints above,
   And in him is God's dwelling place.

Love is a treasure past compare—
   Angels without it, would be poor;
With it, the beggar heaven shall share
   As long as spirit can endure.

'Twas lost by Adam when he fell;
   'Tis gain'd through Jesus crucified;
Let every heart with praises swell,
   Faith, Hope, and Love they still abide.

BE HAPPY.

"Be happy," says the opening morn,
When slum'ring nature wakes to life,
While yet the stars the west adorn,
And night and day hold noiseless strife.

CHORUS.

Be happy, be happy, the voice universal
I hear it at morn, at noon, and at night;
All nature unites in its constant rehearsal
Inviting us mortals in God to delight.

"Be happy," says the fervent noon,
When vig'rous life is on the wing,
When all but man join in the tune,
Which all beside him ever sing.
    Chorus.

"Be happy," says the closing day,
While angels' pencils touch the sky,
With azure, gold and purple ray,
And all the hues of nature's dye.
    Chorus.

"Be happy," says the solemn night,
When nature's pulse but faintly beats,
When twinkling stars with modest light,
Or Luna's ray the optic greets.
    Chorus.

The roaming beasts o'er hill and dale,
The feathered minstrels of the wood,
The insect tribes or ponderous whale,
With all the tenants of the flood;
    Chorus.

The mountains, vales, and rivers all,
The gurgling brook and ocean's tide,
Niagara in its thundering "Fall,"
And all the cascade world beside;
    Chorus.

The vine, the bush, and stately tree,
The hail, and snow, and teaming rain;
All things we taste, feel, hear, or see,
"Be happy," say in accents plain.
    Chorus.

But nature's God, in boundless love,
To make our happiness secure,
A message from His throne above
Hath sent on Lips divinely pure.
    Chorus.

"Come weary, heavy laden come,
My easy yoke and burden bare,
Then share with me my heavenly home,
Eternal rest with angels share."

CLOSING CHORUS.

Be happy, be happy, the voice universal,
Saints, angels, and Jesus, in concert I hear,
The music of nature in constant rehearsal,
God's message of love our sad spirits to cheer.

TRIFLES.

Whist! hearken husband, listen wife,
'Tis trifles make the sum of life;
From rain and dew-drops rivers flow,
" Tall oaks from little acorns grow."
So penny trifles build our wealth,
And temperance trifles give us health.
Words are trifles, but when spoken,
Hearts by them are heal'd or broken.
Smiles are trifles, but a treasure
Lies within them rich with pleasure.
Neglected trifles often prove
A hindrance to our mutual love;
Nail or screw by "Will." Neglected,
Brings him trouble unexpected;
And so of many trifles more—
A broken pane or unhing'd door.
Then, William, mind each trifling thing,
For trifles joy or sorrow bring.
A stitch's a trifle, but a crime
If 'tis neglected in its time;
And may require a score or two,
When now a single one would do

How much ill-feeling may arise
From trifles, with their sightless eyes,
Neglected from the husband's shirt—
'Tis the neglect his feelings hurt.
Then mind your trifles, Mary Ann,
And ever try to please the man.
If either do a trifle wrong
Haste to correct it—don't prolong
The time—now, this very minute—
Years of sorrow may be in it.
Then both of trifles have a care:
Of what you eat, and drink, or wear;
Of what you think, act, look, or speak.
Be Daniel wise, and Moses meek;
Be Deb'rah brave, and Mary pure,
Christ-like, and constant bliss secure.
Invoke the morn to quicken thought
To mind your trifles as you ought;
Ask of the noon with beaming light,
If your trifles all are right;
Invite the evening shades to tell
If you've mark'd your trifles well;
And if you find your trifles right,
Blest shall you both be, day and night.

GREAT THINGS.

Permit, kind friends, an aged Bard—
Who, battling with the world, is scarr'd
    From heel to crown,
And still is doing battle fair
With hosts of ills, led by despair
    With fearful frown—

To speak a word, though by proxy;
'Tis not now quite orthodoxy
    For Bard to meet
At festive boards, with Pleasure's throng,
To tune his harp, or trill his song,
    Though e'er so sweet.

Permitted! First to him whose duty
Manhood joins to Love, and Beauty,
    Advice I give:
O tie the bands of Hymen strong,
That they may hold the parties long
    As both shall live.

Next the Bridegroom, WILLIAM MOODY,
In vig'rous Manhood, strong and ruddy,
    I will address;
And then the smiling, blushing Bride,
Who takes her place close at his side
    In wedding dress.

Once on a time I TRIFLES wrote,
But now conclude to change my note,
    And GREAT THINGS sing;
For great the Parson's duty is
To make two one, and seal their bliss
    With marriage ring.

And great the interchange of vows,
Between the Husband, and the Spouse,
    They freely make;
And great their mutual duties now,
To truly keep, that sacred vow
    'Till death shall break.

Great is the world of Joy, and Woe,
And great the throng who onward go
    Toward the goal;
And great the scenes which there transpire,
Which some may dread,—others desire
    With tranquil soul.

In reference to that final scene,
There are no TRIFLES here I ween,
　　But all are GREAT;
The smile, the word, the thought, act, look,
Are all recorded in that Book—
　　The Book of Fate.

If all are great, then sure we may
This scene upon this festive day
　　Call greater still,—
The greatest of the acts of life,—
When two become Husband and Wife
　　By God's own will!

Great pleasure may you all enjoy;
Nor let the Bard your mirth destroy
　　With truthful song;
He would not damp, but to secure
The joys which ever shall endure
　　Your being long.

I wish to you, the Happy Pair,
A period long of pleasures rare
　　In your new state;
And may your study ever be,
Each with the other to agree
　　In counsel sweet.

May ne'er the bane of marriage state—
INDIFFERENCE to each other's fate—
   Be your sad lot!
But constant SYMPATHY impart
A pleasure to each other's heart,
   Nor once forgot.

O may we all each other greet
In that bright world, where Saints shall meet
   At God's right hand!
And swell the notes of endless praise,
To the GREAT SAVIOUR of our race,
   In every land.

A FRAGMENT.

The precious Bible is my book,
For comfort oft to it I look;
O, may it ever guide my feet,
To Jesus, and His mercy seat.

WHISKY DEVIL IS HIS NAME.

I was happy, he was cheerful,
Children laugh'd in playful glee,
He my husband, they his likeness,
With the baby on his knee.

O, what pleasant days pass'd by us,
Peace and plenty all the while;
But a demon spirit enter'd—
Fell of purpose, cruel, vile.

Soon he sour'd my husband's temper,
Peace he drove in wrath away,
Plenty then was bid to follow,
Joy, without them, could not stay.

All, alas! is sorrow, sadness,
Since the cruel monster came;
Such a monster, oh! how cruel,
WHISKY DEVIL is his name.

Now our children cry with hunger,
Now they shiver with the cold,
Now their clothes all hang in tatters,
Every thing for rum is sold.

O, for mercy's sake, befriend us,
Make a law like that in Maine,
Then once more our home is happy,
For the monster will be slain.

Help us, help us, Mister Printer,
Help us, You who make the laws,
Help us, Voters, help us, Rulers;
'Tis a just and holy cause.

IMPROMPTU ON MARRIAGE.

As meet two streams, and gently flow
In one, through all the plain below;
As sunbeams by the lens unite
In one intense, and burning light,—
So hearts, if pure, both flow and shine,
When wedlock all their powers combine.

BUNKER HILL MONUMENT.

I've seen thee oft—I see thee still,
Proud shaft on Bunker's prouder hill;
I see thee now, though distant far,
And hill and cloud my vision bar;
By night I see thee as by day,
Where'er I am, whene'er I will,
Thy presence is before me still,
And there, must ever stay.

I've seen thee oft—I see thee still,
As I approach thy far-fam'd hill,
Where freemen's sires for freedom bled,
Where Warren found a gory bed,
And England learn'd a fearful truth,
That men for freedom would contend,
Though death to kindred hearts they send,
To aged sires or youth.

I've seen thee oft—I see thee still.
I stand upon thy blood-stain'd hill,
And see thee in thy giant pride,
With thy firm, smooth, unletter'd side,
Thy apex pierces now the sky,
And clouds to right, and left defile;
Thy summit now a granite isle,
Rain here—up there 'tis dry.

I've seen thee oft,—but why not still?
Below me lies the cloud capp'd hill,
Ah! on thy summit now I stand;
When rais'd, we oft o'erlook the hand
Which help'd us in our upward way;
Though elevated to the sky,
Again I have thee in my eye,
'Tis gone,—thou wilt not stay.

I've seen thee oft—I see thee still,
Far off upon the battle hill.
At distance now I wond'ring stand,
And view thee in an aspect grand,
As painted on the canvas'd sky—
A picture pencil ne'er excell'd,
Thy height to the immense is swell'd,
Sublimely towering high.

I see thee now, and ever will,
While freedom points me to that hill,
Remember thee,—where heroes fell;
And to my children's children tell
The tale my grandsire oft hath told:
How England tax'd our glass and tea,
For paper stamp'd requir'd a fee,
And fathers fought so bold.

THE THREE SMILES.

It smiles! What smiles?
      The Babe at the breast,
On whom the cold hand of want never prest,
Who knows naught of earth, its sickness and sorrow,
And never yet dream'd of a dying to-morrow—
        It smiles.

They smile! Who smile?
      The Reckless and Gay,
Whose thoughts are bounded within the short day,
Nor think they, nor care they, for death or old age,
But pleasures, and fashions all their moments engage—
        They smile.

They smile! Who smile?
      The Humble and Wise,
Who think of the grave, and pant for the skies;
They would not live alway in sorrow and pain,
But haste to the kingdom, there with Jesus to reign—
        They smile.

The Babe's smile is but unconscious gladness,
The Reckless and Gay, their smile is but madness,
But the Christian's smile shall never know sadness—
        They truly smile.

CALVARY.

Dark was the storm, and darker still
The night of sorrow in my soul,
When my proud mind, and stubborn will,
Would not submit to God's control,
   But rose in might
   Against the light
Which on me beam'd from Calv'ry's hill.

The billow'd passions ebb'd and flow'd,
On its rough tide all hope was lost,
Temptation's fiercest tempest blow'd,
And all my powers, thus tempest-toss'd
   Shipwreck had made
   Without the aid
Of Calv'ry's light which on me glow'd.

My eye upon that light I plac'd,
Its beams with hope inspir'd my heart,
By it the way of life I trac'd,
And then resolv'd with sin to part;
   'Twas then I knew
   His promise true—
With Calv'ry's light my foes I fac'd.

By that blest ray I'll travel on
Until I gain the world of bliss;
Now every cloud of doubt is gone,
This is my hope, and only this:
   Christ died for me
   On Calvary—
Foundation sure to build upon.

THE FISHERMAN.

Written in a Mrs. Merit's album, under a picture of an old man who was fishing, his basket hanging behind him on a tree.

Have you, dear friend, perus'd the book,
Which WALTON wrote beside the brook,
Of pick'rel, perch, of chub and trout,
And every fish we know about?
The "Complete Angler" is its name,
A work which gave old Izzak fame,
Which critics say for MERIT true,
Was ne'er excell'd by only two
Of all who wrote of every age,
To grace old England's classic page.

The man above, with line and hook,
Methinks is he who wrote the book;
And if it is, I surely wish
"Good luck," a basket full of fish.
And if he has a "mess" to spare,
I hope he'll leave them in your care;
And when I come my friends to see,
I hope you'll cook them all for me.

Thus far the picture is my theme;
But now I turn to say,
As life is passing as the stream,
As transient as the meteor's beam,
Be wise, be wise, to-day;
And seek a treasure in the skies,
Where sacred friendship never dies,
And pleasures ever stay.

SABBATH SCHOOL.

My father is a teacher kind,
He scholars has a plenty,
He prays for all, and talks with each,
Though they are more than twenty.

But I too had a teaching turn,
And lov'd the children's prattle;
I loved to see them uniform,
And hate to lie, and tattle.

The Sabbath came; my father smil'd,
I could not be resisted,
But off I went to Sabbath school,
And as a teacher 'listed.

I taught my class the Gospel way,
Sang tunes, both loud and charming,
But found indeed the teacher's task
Requir'd a heavenly arming—

To meet the foe of God and man,
By Robert Rakes made raving—
Requir'd an arm made strong by grace,
A heart, all dangers braving.

But I am glad that I became
A teacher bold and daring,
By grace prepar'd to meet the foe,
No pains or labor sparing.

MY HOME.

A FRAGMENT.

It stood alone upon a hill,
A lovely little cot,
The nearest was a fulling mill,
If I have not forgot;
Two miles below a pretty church,
Beside a shady grove
Of beach and maple, pine and birch,
A shelter for the drove.
Above, a mountain steep and high
In simple grandeur rose,
Obscuring half the northern sky,
And white with winter's snows;
Far on the left a shining pool,
From thence a rippling brook
Roll'd gently on so clear and cool,
A winding course it took,
Until it reach'd the mill near by,
And then awhile it stay'd,
Until the water rose so high,
That o'er the dam it play'd;
Upon the right the rustling corn,
And pastures fair and green,
Where late at night and early morn,
The farmer boy was seen.
Some other things I now forget;
For long, long time ago,
It is since I and Juliette,
Liv'd in that cot so low.

WHY SHOULD YOU WEEP?

Consolatory lines, addressed to parents who had been bereaved of both of their children.

Why should you weep, fond parents, why?
Your lovely babes can no more die,
They are with Jesus, in His arms,
And smile, and sing with heavenly charms;
Though lovely here, yet lovelier there,
'Midst cherub hosts all shining fair,
Their souls enlarg'd to angel size,
With knowledge vast, like angels wise,
Like angels, pure, like angels, bright—
They shine in robes of living light.

Why should you weep, dear parents, why?
Your smiling babes look from the sky;
They speak, ah! listen, O how sweet,
Angelic tones, 'tis heaven complete,
But list again—'tis Frances E.
Whose months on earth were only three;
She speaks, ah! hear her gently say
" Come, parents dear, come, come away;"
A pause, and then in accents pure,
List! hear! 'tis Angelina sure,

Nine months four days she sojourn'd here,
Then left this clime so dark and drear;
And with Elizabeth she cries,
"Come, come, dear parents, to the skies."

How can you weep, dear Edward, how?
Weep not, but in submission bow,
With dear Elizabeth your spouse,
Remembering all your sacred vows,
Live here for God, then rest above
With those dear babes you fondly love,
And with them sing in heavenly strains,
And walk with them those shining plains,
Where tears, and sighs, and cares are o'er,
And parting scenes are known no more.

We have two babes with your's in bliss,
I hear them sing while writing this;
I hear them speak as oft before,
And bid us weep for them no more;
We will not weep, we will not sigh,
For our dear children in the sky.

BOYS OF SWITZERLAND.

Our cot was shelter'd in a wood,
And by a lake's green margin stood,
A mountain bleak behind us frown'd,
Whose top the snow in summer crown'd;
But pastures fair, and green to boot,
Lay smiling at the mountain's foot,
Here first we frolick'd hand in hand—
Two orphan boys of Switzerland.

When scarcely old enough to know
The meaning of a tale of woe,
'Twas then by mother we were told,
That father in his grave lie cold;
But livelihoods were hard to get,
And we too young to labor yet,
The tears within our eyes did stand—
Two orphan boys of Switzerland.

While yet too young, to plough, or sow,
Or handle shovel, spade, or hoe,
We told kind mother we would try
To sow our field, with wheat, or rye;
But, ah! no seed could we obtain,
For crops had fail'd for lack of rain,
So still we liv'd on fish and bran—
Two half-starv'd boys of Switzerland.

Worn down with grief, poor mother said
"She could no longer earn us bread;
That we must for ourselves provide,
And plough the ocean's stormy tide."
But, ah! the anguish we then felt;
Our youthful hearts with grief did melt,
As mother gave the parting hand
To her poor boys of Switzerland.

With throbbing heart, and falling tear,
We left our home, and mother dear,
With haste to Liverpool we went
And shipp'd on board the fated "Kent."
Five hundred souls in all we found,
To Ceylon's coast the ship was bound,
We sail'd, and soon lost sight of land—
Two sailor boys of Switzerland.

The wind a hurricane soon blew,
And swiftly on our vessel flew,
The mountain waves, all capp'd with foam,
Brought sweet remembrance of our home;
But here no pastures green and fair,
No mother's voice to soothe our care,
'Twas "watch and watch" we both must stand,
Two sailor boys of Switzerland.

For many days the storm increas'd,
Though sick, we could not be releas'd;
But run, and pull, aloft, on deck,
At our stern captain's call, and beck.
Amid our toil, and youthful fear
We thought of home, and mother dear,
We seem'd to hear her voice so bland,
Cheering her boys of Switzerland.

The captain's boast, the seaman's pride,
"Our noble ship" the storm defied,
From wave, to wave, she track'd her way,
Through fields of foam, and showers of spray
And though around 'twas dark, and drear,
Hope banish'd every rising fear;
As safe, as though by zephyrs fann'd
We felt, brave boys of Switzerland.

The storm increas'd for six long days,
Nor sun, nor moon, shed forth their rays,
The seventh, at noon, the sun appear'd,
His presence every bosom cheer'd;
And soon we hop'd the sea again
Would change from mountain wave to plain,
And thus we both fair weather plann'd,
Two storm-sick boys of Switzerland.

But towering still the billows roll'd.
Our mate with light went to the "hold;"
Our greatest danger now had come—
A cask had bilg'd, containing rum.
The mate misstepp'd, and dropp'd his light,
Which did at once the rum ignite;
Quick rose the flame, a column grand,
Around us boys of Switzerland.

Now all on board was fear, and dread,
From stem, to stern, the flames soon spread;
A distant ship beheld the flame,
And quickly to our rescue came,
And hundreds by their efforts save,
While many found a watery grave;
But God preserv'd us by His hand—
We orphan boys of Switzerland.

We soon reach'd England's shore again,
Not long, however, to remain;
On board another gallant ship,
Out of the dock we gently slip.
For Canton now our sails are spread,
May Heaven, His blessing, on us shed,
Protect us by His mighty hand,
Mother to see—and Switzerland.

ALBUM KEPT ABOVE.

DEDICATION OF AN ALBUM FOR A LADY.

There is an album kept above,
On its first page is written, LOVE,
By Him, Who was the sinner's Friend,
Whose love is boundless, knows no end.
On pages of that Album fair,
Stands every name who enters there.
May yours, dear DORA, stand with those
Who now are friends, but once were foes
To Him, Who, with His blood did trace,
Love, dying love, for all our race.
May all, whose words of friendship true,
Shall here be found inscrib'd to you,
And all, who on this page shall look,
With him, who dedicates this book,
Be written there, on Life's fair page,
With those, of every, clime and age.

ON THE DEATH
OF THE HON. THOMAS D'ARCY McGEE,
April 10, 1868.

We saw thee oft—we see thee still,
As once thou stood'st, on freedom's hill,
A conqu'ring chieftain, firm and bold,
Clad, in the statesman's armor bright—
To meet the enemies of right—
Stronger than they a thousand fold.

We saw thee oft—we see thee still;
But not upon the battle hill,
With helmet, buckler, shield and sword;
For death, thy foe,—a friend hath come,
A messenger, to call thee home,
To find in heaven, thy great reward.

We saw thee oft—we see thee still—
Thy presence comes without the will,
But choice, detains, our welcome guest;
We listen to the notes of praise
Which lips, immortal, ever raise
In that eternal land of rest.

We see thee now, a conqu'ror crown'd,
Midst hosts of conqu'rors clust'ring round;
And foremost, in that shining crowd,
We see thy compeers here in arms,
With crowns of life, and conqu'ring palms,
They raise the song of triumph loud.

O'Connell, Emmet, press thee near,
Tone, Holt, and Grattan too, appear,
And all the Irish, patriot band
Whom, God hath call'd from earth away
To their reward, in endless day,
With such, of every age, and land.

To see thee, Plunkett shouts anew,
Fitzgerald, Burke, and Devereux;
O'Donnel, Curran, Flood, O'Shea,
McNevin, Russell,—all unite
To welcome thee, to realms of light—
Our, honor'd, lov'd, and fam'd McGee.

We've seen thee in a bloodless strife
Do battle, to the end of life,
And seal, thy mission, with thy blood!
McGee—" Peacemaker," " Patriot," " Friend "—
We deeply mourn thy tragic end,
And grief-drops, mingle in a flood.

Soon, will thy sacred house of clay,
To the cold tomb, be borne away,
To wait the trump, of God, to sound;
Then rising from thy dusty bed,
With Christ, our risen, glorious head,
May we who live, with thee, be found.

IMPROMPTU ON HEARING OF McGEE'S DEATH.

The whole Dominion weeps for thee,
Our honor'd, much lov'd friend, McGee,
Could sighs, and tears, thy life restore
We'd see thee in our midst once more;
But sighs, and tears, alas! are vain,
McGee—we ne'er shall see again.

Our country mourns—McGee is dead!
And o'er his bier, we freely shed
The drops of deepest sorrow;
A star, of the first magnitude—
A noble statesman, wise and good—
Will be entomb'd to-morrow!

THE SABBATH.

Blest Sabbath, 'tis a day of rest,
A day to treasure up for heaven;
The Spirit's power is felt to bless
Alike, on this, as all the seven.

This hallow'd day inspires the soul
With thoughts sublime, of Christ, our God;
Our spirits yield to love's control,
And in affliction, own, His rod.

In prayer, and praise, we raise our voice,
Our hearts, aspire in solemn awe,
Thy courts, are made our willing choice,
To pay our vows, and hear Thy law.

O! glorious type, of perfect rest,
Where, the soul's Sabbath ne'er shall end,
Where praise shall swell, and prayer shall cease,
And saints, enjoy the sinner's Friend.

TO TWO YOUNG MISSIONARIES.

Brothers, what fired your youthful souls
To leave this land of truth, and light,
To go, where Sen'gal's waters roll,
Where heathen dwell, in moral night?

Why have you left your parents dear,
Your brothers, sisters, friends, and home,
And drawn from all the parting tear—
On Afric's, barren sands to roam?

Was it to find the golden ore,
Or gather diamonds on the coast,
To treasure up a costly store,
And in your wealth return, to boast?

" O, no!" in warmth, I hear you say;
" 'Twas not for wealth we left our land,
To spend the long meridian day
On Afric's, burning, sterile sand;

" But 'twas for this, and this alone—
To preach, to them, a Saviour's love,
To tell them, God, in Christ will own
And bring them to His courts above—

"Tell them in language heaven inspires,
Ethiope shall stretch forth her hand,
And raise to God, their hearts' desires,
While mercy hovers o'er their land.

" To raise their minds from nature's night,
To teach them science, reason, law,
Teach them the fight, of Faith, to fight,
And cease the bloody sword to draw.

" O, may we but these objects gain,
And Christianize our sable friends,
We'll welcome, sorrow, want, and pain,
And toil, till life's short journey ends."

PRISONER OF HOPE.

Prisoner of hope, fresh courage take;
Be not dismay'd, but travel on;
The world, the flesh, and all forsake,
For soon you'll be, where Christ is gone.

Trust, then, in Jesus, humble saint,
And, hoping, press the prize to gain;
Weary, you need not be, or faint,
But win, though in the conflict slain.

THE DYING YEAR—1866.

The dying year, how loud its voice
To mortal man, " Prepare,"
Demands of him, the instant choice,
Repentance, faith, and prayer.

The youth, by it, is urg'd to flee
The way of mirth and pride,
And humbly bend the willing knee
To Jesus crucified.

The middle-ag'd, are call'd to spend
The vigor of their days
In duties, which shall only end
When prayer, shall end in praise.

To age, the call is louder still;
Demands, without delay
Submission, to their Maker's will
Before another day.

To all, it speaks in thunder tone,
And says, " To-day be wise,
To-day, your God, your Saviour, own,
Now, ere this moment flies."

The clock has struck the hour of ten,
Fast dying is the year,
Two hours remain, and noiseless then
The *New One* may appear.

But thousands now, who hope to see
The first of sixty-seven,
Will be in vast eternity,
In hell, or blissful heav'n!

STREAM OF LIFE.

The stream moves on with steady flow,
And seeks its level far below,
Nor tarries then, for in the ocean,
It still moves on, and never rests,
But 'midst the billowy commotion
From north to south, from east to west,
Moves ever, to and fro.

The stream of life, soon, soon will end
And death shall sever friend, from friend,
But for a season—shall it be;
For yonder, in that ocean vast,
Eternity's unbounded sea
Greeting of friends, shall ever last,
And pleasures never end.

K

BREAK-HEART HILL.

I am not positive that the following narrative of the Maiden of Break-Heart Hill is as the facts were related. I write from memory, and have given them nearly, I think, as I had them from a friend in Ipswich.

In Ipswich, Massachusetts, is a hill, called Break-Heart, which derived its name from the circumstance of a maiden of Ipswich, who sat on its brow a part of each day, and sometimes whole days together, for many months, watching for the signal of her lover, who was captain of a war vessel belonging to the English navy during the war of the Revolution. He had been ordered to another station for a season, and expected to return in a few months and marry the lady. He was to give a particular signal, which she looked for in vain, for he fell in battle, and she, from disappointment and exposure, sickened, pined away, and died.

On a lone cliff, where surges roughly beat,
   A maiden wander'd with a troubl'd soul.
No noble ship her steady gaze did greet,
   And onward still, the stormy waves did roll.

For many months, she sought the ocean's side,
   And morn, and noon, and night, with anxious eye,
She gaz'd to see, upon the briny tide,
   Her William's ship, then gave the heartfelt sigh.

Twice had the sun, his northern tropic seen,
  Since her dear lover left her fond embrace,
Yet, on the cliff, she every day had been;
  Through snow, and sleet, you might her footsteps trace.

Though others had no hope, yet her fond heart,
  Still hop'd in frenzy, bord'ring on despair;
And when she slept, she in her dreams would start,
  And cry, He comes! he comes! I see him there!

He came not ever, but in battle fell;
  But death soon came, and set her spirit free;
And where her body lies, many will tell,
  If you to Ipswich go, and wish to see.

In memory of the maiden, and her woe,
  They call it Break-Heart Hill, where once she sigh'd.
The very rock where lone she sat, they show,
  On which she gladly would have lain and died.

LET ME GO.

"Let me go! let me go!" the words of the dying,
  The spirit all plum'd, for a flight, to the skies;
But fetters of earth on its pinions were lying,
  As upward to glory it waited to rise.

There came a bright angel, from God, with the token,
  That now all those fetters aside should be laid—
The silver cord loosen'd, the golden bowl broken;
  Then joyful, the summons, the spirit obey'd.

O'er the clay remaining, in anguish were bending
  The lov'd ones, who wept, that life's last sands were run;
They heard not the song, of the freed soul ascending,
  They saw not the crown, and the rest it had won!

Weep not for the dust, that in darkness must moulder,
  Consign'd in its freshness, and bloom to the sod;
The cold arms of death, shall soon cease, to enfold her,
  And give back their trust in the likeness of GOD.

But where the destroyer, ne'er wing'd his dread arrow,
  And tears never fall, for the early deplor'd—
Beyond the dark grave, and its portals so narrow,
  You shall meet, the lov'd, at the feet of her LORD!

INSTALLATION HYMN.

Composed for the occasion of Installing Rev. S. Remington, as Pastor over the Village Baptist Church, Fitchburg, Mass., 1846.

Eternal Father! source of love!
Incline thine ear in mercy now,
And grant the blessing from above,
For which, we at thy altar bow.

God of the sacramental host!
Send down thy pure baptismal flame,
As on the day of Pentecost
When thousands bow'd to Jesus' name.

On this, thy servant, pour thine oil;
His great commission, now renew,
That he with willing heart may toil,
Proclaiming all thy gospel true.

As the good shepherd leads his sheep
In pastures green, by waters still;
So may he lead, and ever keep
This flock, from every threat'ning ill.

May sinners tremble at thy word,
Which he shall faithfully declare,
And hundreds, soon in praise, be heard,
Who here, shall in thy mercy share.

And when his voice is heard no more,
And dust, to dust, shall turn again;
May he on Canaan's blissful shore,
With this dear people ever reign.

Command thy blessing now on all
Who wait in faith, thy power to feel,
And on thy servant, we INSTALL,
Place thou thine own eternal seal!

CHILD AND FLOWER.

How fading are all earthly things!
Each joy, its train of sorrow brings;
Pain follows ease; tears follow joys,
And Death, the brightest hope destroys.

I've seen the flower of choicest bloom
Wither, beside a lov'd one's tomb;
No more its beauty blest the sight,
No more its fragrance gave delight.

I saw that loved one, bright and fair,
A child he was of beauty rare;
But Jesus, sent His angel band,
Who bore him to a fairer land—

A land where all is life, and joy,
Where the freed spirit finds employ,
In hymning songs, of sweeter tone
Than angel's harps, have ever known.

Unlike the flower, which lives no more,
Your lov'd one lives, on life's blest shore;
And when you reach that heavenly plain
That son, shall smile on you again!

Dry, then, those tears,—why should you weep
For one, whom Love Divine shall keep—
A treasure, purchas'd with the blood
Of the dear, suffering, Son of God?

TO MY SISTER HANNAH.

Dear sister Hannah, should a tear
Fall from thy brilliant eye,
Thou hast a friend, warm, and sincere,
In him, 'twill cause a sigh.

Should pleasure on thy visage play,
And health, and wealth attend,
Pleasure to him it will convey,
Who always is your friend.

Where'er, kind Providence directs,
May you submissive go,
Safe, if His mighty hand protects,
On Afric's sand, or Greenland's snow.

The blank remaining in your book,*
Expresses what I can't reveal,
I have not chang'd in thought, or look,
Though you have chang'd, to " Teel."

Excuse my rhyme, and metre too,
Excuse all faults likewise;
Regard me now, as ever, true
Till death dissolve the ties.

* I asked the favor to write in her book,
She smiled like an angel, and said " Yes," with a look:
Then I wrote as I felt, and felt as I wrote,
And a blank, with my name, was the whole of my note.

GO, DEAR GIRL.

To the same; on her leaving home for a distant land.

Go, dear girl, where fortune leads you,
With the blessing of a friend,
Trust in God, Who daily feeds you,
He will all your steps attend.

Go to distant lands a stranger,
Far from friends, who love you dear,
O'er the ocean, fear no danger,
God is there, as well as here.

When, far off, your feet shall wander,
May your paths, be paths, of peace,
While on pleasures past you ponder,
May bright hope your joys increase.

If we ne'er again shall mingle
In the social circle sweet,
Hearts like ours, cannot be single,
But as one, shall ever beat.

Must I shed the tear of anguish,
Must I give the parting hand,
Must I here in sorrow languish,
While you roam a distant land?

Go, sweet girl, the word is spoken;
Go, you must, 'tis duty's call;
Go, but take this simple token,
Wet with tears, which freely fall!

ON A DEAR BROTHER.

O may the green turf lightly press
That lovely, manly, youthful form;
That heart, and hand, so prompt to bless,
While erst with life, and feeling warm.

Thou need'st no monumental stone,
Thy merits to emblazon forth,
For all to whom thy name is known,
Are living records of thy worth.

Thy bosom was the hallow'd shrine
Of justice, charity, and truth;
In thee, did every virtue shine,
And every grace, adorn'd thy youth.

Friendship with thee, was not a name—
A flickering light, by interest fed;
But as sublime, and pure a flame
As burns around a seraph's head.

Philanthropy, it fill'd thy soul
With love, for all the human race,
And could thy arms have clasp'd the whole,
The whole, had shar'd, thy warm embrace.

But, ah! thou'rt gone, on earth no more
Shall we behold our much-lov'd friend,
Hope bids us seek thee, on that shore
Where death can't sever, bliss can't end.

WATER HILL.

A TUNE OF MY OWN COMPOSING.

Free from the busy scenes of life,
The noise of war, the senate's strife,
The empty sound of rising fame,
And heroes, bleeding for a name—
Grant me, O Powers Supreme, a place
Where all those jarring tumults cease,
Have just enough to bear me o'er
The stage of life, not rich, or poor;
But blest, amid some rural scenes,
Of purling streams, and flowery greens,
Enraptur'd rove, and there enjoy
What man can't give, and can't destroy.

What music is it strikes my ear,
And all my powers in raptures thrill,
Ah! me, it is our Lucy dear,
Chanting the tune, call'd, " Water Hill."

She pours it forth in melting strains,
In notes so full, and smooth, and shrill,
It surely every passion chains,
That lovely tune, call'd, " Water Hill."

I've wish'd for months that song to hear,
Its rural scenes and purling rill,
But little thought the time so near,
To hear her lips sing "Water Hill."

At morn, or noon, or dusky eve,
When all is noise, or hush'd and still,
My ear is ready to receive
The charming notes of "Water Hill."

If passion rages in my breast,
Or sorrow, my poor heart should fill,
Nought will restore my wonted rest
Like soothing, melting "Water Hill."

Music, 'tis said, "The Lion chains,"
It chains the lion of the will,
Powerless am I, to hear those strains,
Blended so sweet in "Water Hill."

THE RETURNED FAIR ONE.

Long days, and months have roll'd away,
Since her departure from our home,
Nor longer could dear Lucy stay,
But, wild with joy, she's smiling come.

Sarah rejoic'd to hear her voice,
And Abigail, with pleasure smil'd,
Phedora blush'd, the Fair one's choice,
And Samuel, with joy was wild.

From morn till noon, from noon till night,
Her voice in sweetest music broke,
Her countenance, so fair, and bright,
Still sweeter, than her language spoke.

Though cold had been the winter's day,
Yet lovely spring with her return'd,
December was as bright as May,
The fire itself, more briskly burn'd.

And has she come, to go again,
Again, again, so soon to part,
Must pleasure yield, so soon, to pain,
And wake the sorrows of the heart?

Yes, she must go, and say " good bye,"
To those dear friends who love her well;
The girls will weep, the boy will sigh,
And all will feel, what none can tell.

FOR AN ALBUM.

To friendship sacred, and to love,
This little volume shines,
May thrills of joy your bosom move
When you peruse its lines.

May no unhallow'd, trifling themes
Its pages e'er disgrace,
No fancy's fleeting, fading dreams
Within it find a place.

May true affection, here express'd,
Pleasure impart to thee,
And on its pages ever rest
Refin'd simplicity.

Devoted to your happiness,
May all your friends prove true,
And here permit me to express
The love I feel for you.

And when these pages you review,
And this shall meet your sight,
Be pleased, its meaning to construe
In love, then all is right.

FRIENDSHIP.

Written at the age of fourteen.—1818.

When blest with health, and prospects fair,
We pluck from nature's rich parterre,
The choicest flowers, which blossom there,
      How blest with friendship.

But when with wasting sickness pale,
We find no pleasures in the vale,
And all our fairest prospects fail,
      Then dear is friendship.

If foes unite to do us harm,
With bitter words and threats alarm,
How highly then we prize the arm
      Of constant friendship.

O! friendship, friendship, heavenly name,
Sure from the skies to earth it came;
Better than honor, wealth, or fame,
      Is sacred friendship.

Friendship, thou balm of earthly woes,
And solace to the troubled breast,
It melts the heart of stoutest foes,
And by this tie we all are blest.

Friendship, thou daughter of the sky,
Sweet aid to happiness below,
Within thine arms, O let me lie,
And never from thy bosom go.

I hate ambition's haughty pride,
And griping avarice I hate,
Friendship my portion, trust, and guide—
Let friendship ever on me wait.

A THOUGHT.

How sweet to think on those we highly prize,
To whom we're bound by friendship's sacred ties;
How long, and tedious, is the halting year,
The days as weeks, and months as years appear,
When those we love, we anxious wait to see,
We wish weeks hours, and years, as weeks to be.

We think of those we love, beyond the tomb,
And hope to see them in eternity,
Then death is robb'd at once of half its gloom,
We pant to see that clime, from sorrow free,
And meet those friends, deck'd in immortal bloom.

THE MONUMENT.

Unletter'd pile, rehearse thy tale,
Why thou dost stand in giant pride,
'Mid storms of thunder, wind, and hail,
Which rush against thy naked side,
Why wilt thou stand in silence there;
To us, to all, thy hist'ry hide.

But, hark! a voice of awful sound,
Like mutt'ring thunder rolls along;
It rends the air, and shakes the ground,
It moves a mighty tempest strong,
And speaks of " Tumult, blood, and fire,
A nation's right, and nation's wrong."

Ah! now I read thy hist'ry plain,
Thou art a monument of war,
How men oppress'd, threw off the chain,
And curs'd oppression did abhor,
And view'd the boon of liberty,
A blessing, worth contending for.

WISH I HAD NEVER BEEN BORN.

IMPROMPTU ON HEARING A YOUNG LADY SAY "SHE WISHED SHE HAD NEVER BEEN BORN!"

Would'st thou be happy, and be blest
With peace of mind, and constant rest,
Obey the voice of sober truth,
And seek religion in youth.
Make Christ your choice, His kingdom gain,
And let your lips, His praise proclaim;
Conform your life to all His laws,
With all your heart, espouse His cause.
At home, abroad, where'er you be,
Remember, Jesus died for thee;
With cheerful smile, and calm content,
Your years in pleasure shall be spent;
And when your span of life is o'er,
And golden moments all are gone,
You'll reign with Christ for evermore,
And praise Him that you e'er *was born*.

NEW ENGLAND CONFERENCE.

Lines on an annual conference of the M. E. Church, in Lynn, Mass.

The seasons, they have roll'd around,
And measur'd off the toilsome year:
Again we've met, on sacred ground
To bless, and soothe, with smile, and tear.

Yes, sacred ground, where Asbury met,
For the first time, that faithful band;
Who toiled, through heat, and cold, and wet,
To cultivate Emmanuel's land.

Yes, where they met, in holy zeal;
New England Conference meets again;
They form'd it then, and fixed its "Seal;"
It lives,—but none of them remain!

Then one, that small—the field was wide;
Now five, each large,—the field the same;
From northern lakes, to ocean's tide,
Connecticut, to State of Maine.

Here Asbury, Allen, Casden, Lee,
Raynor, and Smith, in counsel sweet;
With burning zeal, in harmony,
Their Conference business did complete.

Then not a score, but hundreds now
Preach the dear Saviour, through the land:
And tens of thousands with us bow
In praise, and prayer, at God's command.

May zeal, and love, in us increase;
The love of souls, our spirits fire:
And when we from our labor cease
To Jesus go—our heart's Desire.

Another year of toil, and care,
Hath mov'd in rapid flight away,
But God hath listen'd to our prayer,
And lengthen'd out, our life's short day,
Again in Conference to appear,
And bless Him, for the bygone year.

He hath our many wants supplied;
Upheld us with His gracious hand
While we have wander'd far, and wide,
To cultivate Emmanuel's land;
To scatter seed, both far and near,
And reap, the harvest of the year.

We've seen backsliders turn to God
And give, we trust, their wand'rings o'er :
Unfaithful souls, have felt His rod,
And trembling, fled, to mercy's door ;
And thousands, who had " Ears to hear,"
Have bowed to Christ, within the year.

IMPROMPTU ON A WORDY DEBATE ON TEMPERANCE.

Never, never, O how fearful ;
Never, can we all unite
In one idea, free, and cheerful,
If that idea, should be right.
Milton says, in world of sorrow,
" Spirits damn'd, sweet concord hold."
If such concord, we could borrow,
And for truth, be firm, and bold ;
Soon we'd conquer all our foes,
None would stand the truth to oppose.

ADVICE TO A LAD.

Henry, be good, and love the Lord,
Study, and learn, His holy Word;
Shun every sinful path, and snare,
By seeking God, with fervent prayer.

Chose those who love the way of truth
To be companions of your youth;
And never fear, but to offend
The God of Love, your constant Friend.

Honor, and love, your parents dear;
For you, they've shed the parent's tear;
For you, they've spent the night of care;
For you, they've wrestled long in prayer.

When they are old, their hearts make glad,
And to their comfort, daily add:
So, shall you please, the God of Grace,
And to your life, add many days.

TEMPERANCE SONG.

Husbands, wives, fathers, mothers,
Sons and daughters, sisters, brothers,
Met again to talk and sing,
And make the Hall of Temperance ring
To help each other in the "cause"
By moral suasion, not with laws.

Let us hear from one, and all
A speech against King Alcohol:
Let him in any dress appear—
Rum, gin, cider, brandy, beer;
Thus help each other in the "cause"
By moral suasion, not with laws.

Ladies, sing a temperance song,
And cheer us in our work along;
Draw us on to do our duty
Not alone with love, and beauty:
Help us in our sacred "cause"
With lip persuasion, not with laws.

Soon, the victory shall be won,
Temperance' star, shall blaze a sun
To illumine every land;
Then we'll shout a happy band,
And sustain the Temperance "cause"
With moral suasion, and with laws.

AN EPISTLE TO MY ELDEST DAUGHTER AND HER HUSBAND.

Dear Sarah, and James, I am living as yet,
Though I think oftentimes, my sun will soon set,
If I live to the two-and-twentieth of June,
I shall have passed, by one year, my century's noon.
A long period indeed, of sorrow, and care;
Which has wrinkled my brow, and whitened my hair;
Which learned me true wisdom, by mercy divine,
I've a bright hope of heaven, "For Jesus is mine."
May you, my dear children, think much of my Friend,
Whose mercy is constant, Whose love knows no end.
His presence, now brightens my dark hours of life,
Though depriv'd of dear parents, children, and wife;
And Who in death's vale, 'midst its darkness and gloom,
Will lighten my pathway, and sweeten my tomb,
He's your father's dear Friend, then love Him for this;
When life shall have passed, we will share in His bliss.

I love the old Bible; I read with delight
Its truths, in the morning, at noon, and at night.
From February the ninth, eighteen fifty-three,
To Judith's birthday, the last one that she see;
Three times, have I read, every chapter, and line,
And every day felt, its Great Author was mine.

In the thirteen short days, from last March the third,
I read it again, every chapter, and word,
Now for the fifth time, I am reading with care,
The old, blessed Bible, with watching, and prayer.
I work hard, earn little, but will not complain,
For others work harder, in weakness, and pain,
And get less than my little, yet are content,
Though at the year's end, every dollar is spent;
While I have laid by three hundred, perhaps more,
With a prospect this year to double my store.

I now live in fine style, as soon you will see,
No cakes, and no pies, neither coffee, nor tea,
No eggs, and no meat, neither cabbage, nor peas;
But simply my apples, bread, butter, and cheese:
In addition to this, my short "bill of fare,"
I name but two others, cold water, and air.
I sleep calmly, seven hours, in each twenty-four,
So soundly, I question, if even I snore.

I fear, my dear children, your patience will tire,
So briefly, will say, I have not a desire
For many a thing, which was once my delight,
And deprive myself of them,—am I not right?
For my health, as a whole, is better by far,
Then when fed from frying-pan, kettle, and jar.

I dress like a gentleman, though I am poor;
Which tailors will not complain of, I am sure,
If they get their pay, and ask quite a "round" price,
They care not, how costly I dress, or how nice.

I meddle with politics so far, I think
As will overthrow Popery, Slavery, and Drink.
No farther than this, and I have a good hope,
America ne'er will be ruled by the Pope!

I still read much beside, the Precepts of Truth,
The speeches of Webster, of Mann and Kossuth;
And other great men, who are living, or dead
Who stand, or have stood, at humanity's head.

I study the arts, and find Pleasure Therein,
From the tubular bridge, to a needle or pin.
Am still fond of science, and often at night,
I view the fair moon, and the stars, with delight;
Does a comet appear; or lights of the pole;
Do lightnings flash forth, or the hoarse thunder roll;
It is then, I'm all eye, or else, I'm all ear;
For both give me pleasure, to see, or to hear.
I rove with the botanist o'er the green field,
And pluck herbs, whose virtues, their thousands have
    heal'd,

I talk with the chemist, and curious things learn,
Of simples, and compounds, that freeze, or that burn.
Dear James and S.,—since I last saw your faces,
I have seen many things, and wonderful places;
To tell you of which, I must write a large book,
Much larger, than Izzak's, he wrote by the brook.
I've seen the great ocean, and rivers and lakes,
Niagara too, with its thunders, and quakes.
I have seen tow'ring mountains, wonderful high,
Whose heads seem'd to rear themselves up to the sky;
And other great wonders, I will not relate
In verse, or in prose; will you patiently wait
'Till I see you again, and then I will tell
What I now, cannot, with my pen, quite as well?

I've seen the three kingdoms, and also their kings,
The LION, and the OAK, and GOLD DIAMOND rings.
And queens I have seen, not Queen Vic. but queen Bee—
The good Queen of England, I yet hope to see.

Two other large kingdoms, I've tried to explore
With which, I have had some acquaintance before;
The kingdom of error, and kingdom of truth;
I made quite a study, while yet but a youth.
But new things I learn, and I press on anew,
Erring oft, thinking false things certainly true.

I make many good friends, but seldom a foe;
I speak, and act, kindly, to high, and to low.
I love all mankind, and I pity them too,
For all need our pity—no doctrine more true.

I think of my friends, and I love them much more,
Then ever I have in my lifetime before;
And when I again, in their circle unite,
To make them all happy, I'll strive day and night.

I now wish pleasant dreams, and bid you good night,
Requesting you both a long letter to write
To one who still loves you, and thrice every day,
Does, and will, for your health, and prosperity pray.

I have written above lines a hundred and four;
Please write me as many, and balance the "score."
Believe me as ever, your father, and friend;
So here, my dear children, my letter must end.

A HYMN.—Rom. xiii. 12.

Awake from thy slumbers, 'tis time to arise;
Ere light of eternity, burst on thy sight;
The glory, of Jesus, shall lighten the skies,
And scatter the darkness, that shrouds thee in night.

Awake, from thy slumbers, ye careless, and vain;
Long blinded by Satan, and rul'd by his power;
O haste from his thraldom, and break from his chain,
For Jesus is ready, and now is the hour.

O come to the Saviour; ye wanderers come;
His arms are extended, He bids you return;
O haste to His bosom, the penitent's home;
Of Him who was lowly, humility learn.

Awake from thy slumbers, ye chosen of God;
Rest not on the road, to Emmanuel's land;
The path you are trav'ling, the Saviour once trod,
"The night is far spent, and the day is at hand."

CONSECRATION.

I saw an altar rear'd for prayer,
I long'd to make an offering there,
    A living sacrifice;
But Satan came and show'd me gold,
Of pleasures, fame, and honors told,
    And bid me these to prize.

I turn'd disgusted from them all,
And listen'd to the Spirit's call,
    Who bid me offer now!
By faith His cleansing power to claim,
By faith alone in Jesus' name,
    To God the Father bow.

In agonizing prayer I groan'd,
My wants, and helplessness I own'd,
    But still found no relief;
At last, despairingly, I cried,
Cleanse, Lord, for Thou, for me hast died—
    For me, of sinners chief!

As was my faith, so was I blest,
With perfect love, and perfect rest,
    For all within was pure;
In, and around me, all was God!
On the "Highway thrown up" I trod,
    And every step was sure!

Now sweetly roll my hours away,
'Tis Heaven by night, and bliss by day,
    A Sabbath all the seven.
Tempted, and tried, yet always free,
For in my heart, the sacred Three
    Create a constant Heaven.

Come, every feeble, doubting soul,
Let unbelief no more control,
    But break its cruel chain;
Be strong, be bold—by conqu'ring grace,
Each heart may be the sacred place
    · Where God shall live and reign!

ON AN ANNUAL GATHERING OF CLERGYMEN AND THEIR WIVES.

A year almost hath swiftly fled,
    Since here, a social band, we met;
How many slumber with the dead,
    Whose sun of life, since then, hath set!

Yet we are spar'd, and here we meet
    Our brother, and his household too,
With cheerful hearts, each, all to greet,
    And spend an hour of friendship true.

O, may our hearts in grateful praise,
    Ascend to God, for mercies shown,
Who kindly lengthens out our days,
    And hath our paths with blessings strewn.

Have we been toiling day, and night,
    To cultivate Emmanuel's land—
Scatt'ring the seed by morning light,
    At evening, not withheld our hand—

Not knowing which would prosper most,
    But trusting in the power divine,
That, quicken'd, by the Holy Ghost,
    The barren waste with fruit might shine?

Yes, we have toil'd, and toil we will,
    While we have strength, to preach, or pray,
Fearless we'll stand on Zion's hill,
    And sinners point to Christ, the way.

Have Zion's daughters labor'd too
    In rearing tender plants of grace,
With sacred tears, like evening dew,
    Refreshing every thirsty place?

Yes, they have toil'd, as WOMAN can,
    Blessing with smiles in all our cares,
Aiding, in every holy plan,
    With love, with pity, and with prayers.

And now we've met, a day to spend
    In social conversation sweet;
May Christ, our Saviour, Brother, Friend,
    With us in mercy deign to meet.

May our dear Brother, and his Wife,
    And those lov'd ones, their Children dear,
Be blest, through all the paths of life,
    With grace to comfort, hope to cheer.

May all our days be spent in peace,
    In blessing, and in being blest—
And when our work on earth shall cease,
    May Jesus call us home to rest.

WHY NOT NOW?
Ezek. xxiii. 11.

Why not now? the Father cries,
   As He moves in love to man;
Why neglect to win the prize,
   Since your life is but a span?

Why not now? the Saviour cries;
   Take Me as your only trust,
From your death of sin arise,
   Sav'd from every worldly lust.

Why not now? the Spirit cries,
   Yield thy heart, and all its powers;
By My teachings be made wise—
   Why misspend these golden hours?

Why not now? the preacher cries,
   From the sleep of sin awake;
Plume thy pinions for the skies,
   Every sinful thought forsake.

Why not now? all nature cries,
   Earth, and air, and sea, and sky;
In thy heart, the reason lies—
   Sinners, why not? tell me why.

Will you not? then, dare not blame
    Father, Son, or Holy Ghost,
If you sink in guilt, and shame,
    With the lost, rebellious host.

Will you still go on in sin?
    Stop and think, for death is near;
Now, this moment, now begin
    While the Gospel greets your ear.

Angels look with eager gaze
    On the choice you now shall make;
Will you not their raptures raise,
    And from Satan's bondage break?

Yes, I will, the heart replies,
    I will haste to Jesus now;
While the voice of mercy cries,
    I a penitent will bow.

*   *   *   *   *

Now I feel His pard'ning grace,
    O, what mercy! dying love!
Reconcil'd, the Father's face
    Smiles upon me from above.

Sinners, come! I now can cry—
   Here is mercy, full, and free;
Sinners, turn—why will ye die?
   Jesus died for you and me.

O, the joys my bosom swell!
   Sure, the half was never told;
Angels' tongues could never tell,
   Had they powers a thousand fold.

Here is peace, and joy, and love—
   I had sorrow, pain, and hate;
Here are glories from above,
   Sinners, haste! no longer wait.

By and bye we all shall hear,
   Come, ye blest, or else depart!
Fill'd with love, or rent with fear,
   Will be every human heart.

Joys of heaven, or woes of hell,
   Will be then our endless fate;
Wait no longer! haste and tell
   Others to no longer wait.

THE MOUNT OF SONG.

AN UNFINISHED POEM.

The mount, the glorious mount of song
Hath held spell-bound my spirit long.
I wish'd in childhood's earliest morn,
That I had been, a Poet born,
But soon, I saw the wish was vain,
Content, in age, I dwell the plain
And view that towering mount so high
Whose summit seems to pierce the sky—
And sing of those, whose songs sublime,
Grac'd every age, and every clime.

What multitudes its height to gain
Strove hard, and long, but strove in vain:
Yet still a few, since earth was young,
Have gain'd that height, and proudly sung
Such living strains, that angel's ear
Has caught;—and lowly bent to hear:
Have linger'd long, in raptur'd gaze,
While mortals, sang, immortal lays—
Of God's creative power and skill,
Whose architectural beauties fill

The broad expanse, whose distant shore,
Angels, perhaps, may ne'er explore:
Of earth, and heaven, of death, and hell,
How men, and angels, sinn'd and fell :
Of all things finite man can know
From Godlike high, to atoms low.

First holy prophets touch'd the lyre,
And wrapt a list'ning world in fire ;
And rous'd, the slumb'ring soul to hear
Their notes of love, and hope, and fear,
And thousands now, who sweetly sing,
First caught their strains from prophet's string.

Isaiah sublimely leads the choir ;
He sang the Wonderful Messiah
In strains, which he alone, could sing,
Of sacred song, he reigns the king.
How wrapt, how pure, how graphic too,
His lays for Gentile, and for Jew,
Of Him, Whose stripes, our souls should heal
Whose woes, were for the common weal
And Who alone the wine-press trod
Of the avenging wrath of God!
Though centuries still should intervene,
He wrote, as though the tragic scene

Of Calv'ry's mount, had just transpir'd,
And seeing which, his soul was fired
To sketch the scene, with pencil true,
In sacred light, and shade, and hue,
So plainly, that our sceptic age
Has call'd it a historic page.

*   *   *   *

Next Jeremiah, with plaintive song,
In tears, those sacred strains prolong;
And list'ning earth shall seldom hear
Such notes, impassion'd, terse, and clear;
Like swollen streams, his numbers flow
A mighty song, of Judah's woe!

*   *   *   *

Ezekiel, with his mystic lays;
And David's psalms of rapturous praise,
A Moses, and a Deb'rah's strains,
And others, who on Judah's plains,
Have tun'd the harp, and touch'd the lyre,
And wak'd the soul with sacred fire;
High on the mount, a place have gain'd
Where few above them, ever reign'd;
And where their compeers are but few
From Gentile tribes, or favor'd Jew.

From those inspir'd, we turn our eyes
To hosts, who fain would win the prize,
And drink from the Castilian fount,
And higher climb the sacred mount.
But few alone, of all that throng,
Have climb'd, as high, the mount of song
And fewer, who its summit climbs
With measur'd lays and pleasing rhymes.

Isaiah, of all the bards of yore,
Had one compeer, perhaps no more;
A Homer with heroic strains;
Of uninspir'd, the king he reigns:
Nor can we ever hope to scan
Superiors, to this wond'rous man.
His genius, moulds the thought to form;
His fire, imparts the life-blood warm;
Endows with powers to speak, and move,
Passions to hope, and fear, and love;
His is indeed a model verse,
Simple, descriptive, strong, and terse.

*   *   *   *

Of others, who the lyre hath strung,
Many have well, have sweetly sung.
Distinguish'd by their talents rare
Virgil, and Ovid, praise must share.

Had Homer died when he was young,
Or rather, had he never sung,
Virgil, methinks, had claim'd his place,
For lines of vigor, beauty, grace,
Flow'd from his pen, as rivers flow,
Refreshing all the plains below.
His place is high, by merit higher
Except the king's, than all the choir.

* * * *

A RIDDLE.

I rise early, and late, but seldom retire;
   I can't rise in winter, without a good fire;
I grow, while I'm rising, but stop when I'm up;
   I never eat food, and once only I sup;
I love a good fire, then I'm lively, and light,
   Admir'd by my friends, I'm their constant delight.
No stranger am I, though I tell a strange tale;
   Tell my name, dear children, I think you won't fail.

If you can't "guess" the above—"Cast your bread upon the waters."

SUMMER'S EVE.

The sun it gilds the western sky,
The light recedes, the shades draw nigh,
The clouds are ting'd with nature's dye,
    O lovely summer's eve.

The mind, with care and trouble toss'd,
Weigh'd down with grief, with sorrow cross'd,
Thy beauties then to me are lost—
    Sweet, gentle summer's eve.

But when the trials of the day,
Have been beguil'd by friendship's sway;
'Tis then with pleasure sure I may
    Enjoy the summer's eve.

Along the bank of some smooth stream,
Whose bosom shines with Luna's beam,
I walk, and there on pleasure dream,
    Delightful summer's eve.

But, ah! how short thy longest stay;
December soon succeeds to May,
The lengthen'd night, and shorten'd day—
    Farewell, dear summer's eve.

FRIENDSHIP.

Friendship, thou source of pleasure here,
'Tis thine to wipe away the tear,
To soothe the pain, and calm the fear,
                Blest friendship.

When sorrow bows the spirit down,
And enemies with malice frown,
No other hand with joy can crown
                But friendship's.

When the rough storms of life arise,
And adverse clouds obscure our skies;
'Tis then thine aid we highly prize,
                Sweet friendship.

FOR A MONUMENT.

Creative power, spoke man from dust;
But sin, to dust did man consign;
Redeeming power, in which we trust,
Shall raise again the sacred shrine.

TO A YOUNG CLERGYMAN.

Come, brother, come, prepare your voice
To sound the Gospel clarion shrill;
Say to the sinner, " Make your choice
To-day, and all your vows fulfil."

In melting tones, with fervent soul,
Point them to Calv'ry's victim slain;
Whose blood will make their natures whole,
And wash away, sin's deepest stain.

If this will not affect the heart,
And cause repentant tears to flow:
Point them to Sinai's awful chart—
Then to the burning pool below!

With motives drawn from earth, and hell,
And heaven,—persuade them now to turn,
And dare no longer to rebel,
No longer, heaven, and Jesus spurn.

O awful thought, yet you must tell
The truths of God, in language plain,
The wicked must go down to hell!
To suffer there eternal pain!

Yes, you must speak as God requires,
Nor fear, the face of dying man;
Speak boldly, words which He inspires,
And rescue all the souls you can.

MY TALE IS TOLD.

I'll wander on o'er hill, and dale,
And tell to all my mournful tale;
My tale of truth, though full of grief,
I'll tell,—'twill give my heart relief.

I once had friends, I lov'd them well;
Some true, and others false as hell!

One was a man, who often said,
" Come to my house, my table, bed,
And ever feel that mine, is yours,
As long as waning life endures:"
He from my purse, has largely drawn;
And now I'm poor, he says, " Begone."

Another was a female friend
Who kindly lov'd me to the *End*—
The *End* of wealth, I once possessed;
When poor, she left me with the rest.

Another was a lucky youth
Though sick, and poor, (I speak the truth)
I took him to my home, and there
Bestow'd on him, with kindness rare,
The village school, and then the " High,"
And then to College turn'd his eye,
And when from thence he learned came,
With one of talents, skill, and fame
I paid his bills, three years or more,
While he read Coke, and Blackstone o'er;
I gave to him a lib'ry too
Of volumes rare, both old and new;
And last of all, a place procur'd,
Where he a practice large secur'd;
But now he's rich, and I am poor,
He shuts against me heart, and door!

I had a wife, I lov'd her well,
And she of me the same did tell:
For many years she was my stay,
But death hath taken her away;
And with her, all my children dear,
O'er whom, I long have shed the tear.
For years have fled with rapid haste
Since my last child, a son, I plac'd
In the cold grave; and now alone
I sigh in grief, in pain, I groan.

My parents, brothers, sisters, too,
Have paid the debt, to nature due;
And not a kindred now remains,
Not one, to soothe my woes, and pains.
A poor old man, I trembling stand,
No friend, no kin, no house, no land:
Without a shilling in my purse,
And what to me is still far worse,—
My health is gone, infirm, and old,
My limbs are trembling with the cold!
A pittance give, my wants relieve,
My thanks, and blessing, then receive.

Yet let me add but one word more,
You are the LAWYER, from whose door
With broken heart, I turn'd away
Twelve long years since, this very day:
The "Papers" publish'd me as "dead,"
"He's gone," my neighbors all have said,
But here I stand, sick, weak, and old,
I sink! I sink! MY TALE IS TOLD.

The Lawyer's icy heart did melt,
He humbly to the old man knelt,
Whose falt'ring voice pronounc'd, "Forgive!"
Then clos'd his eyes, and ceas'd to live.

MODERN ISRAEL'S CAPTIVITY AND RELEASE.

Our harps, alas! untuned, unstrung,
    Have long upon the willows hung;
By the cold stream of turbid flow,
    Long have we wept in deepest woe!
Far from the mount of holy song,
    We mourn, and cry, " How long, how long?"

How long, how long, shall Zion weep?
    How long will God His anger keep?
O speed the hour, in mercy speed,
    When Judah's captives shall be freed;
And Zion's Sons their harps shall string,
    And Zion's songs with rapture sing.

But, hark! a voice, 'tis from the skies,
    Jehovah calls, awake, arise;
No longer in thy bondage mourn,
    But to thy native land return;
Thy walls rebuild, thy temple rear,
    And Me alone let Israel fear?

We haste, great God, at Thy command,
    And wend our steps to Zion's land;
Our harps, re-strung, re-tuned again,
    Shall wake in song on Judah's plain,
And vale, and hill-top shall resound,
    From Judah's minstrels all around.

Now safe within thy walls of peace,
    Jerusalem; we will not cease
God's law to love, His will to do,
    And morn and eve our vows renew;
Then God shall our protection be,
    And Israel ever shall be free!

Salvation shall from Zion flow,
    The heathen then our God shall know;
The tribes of earth His power shall own,
    And bow submissive to His throne;
All "kiss the Son," His anger stay,
    And hail the blest millennial day.

A POEM,

WRITTEN FOR HALLOWE'EN, 1866.

Home of our sires, that peaceful land,
   Though distant, yet we love thee still;
Thy forests, lakes, and mountains grand,
   Thy names which hist'ry's pages fill,
Thy manners, usages and arts—
   All, all, we prize with grateful hearts.

We would not damp the feeling strong
   Which binds us to our country dear,
Nor check the sentimental song
   Which prompts the smile or draws the tear;
But arts and science now dispel
   The fairy throng, the magic spell.

To deeper fix on mem'ry's page,
   We meet to keep our Hallowe'en;
Here vig'rous youth, and hoary age,
   With all the ranging years between,
In one great crowd together meet,
   And kindly here each other greet.

No bonfires now with vivid blaze,
   No pealing *bells* salute our ears,
No magic spells, spirits to raise,
   To fill the timid ones with fears;
But fires of love, *true spirits* warm,
   And lovely BELLES with music charm.

The fairy bands we now out-speed,
   With messages of weal or woe,
The swift-wing'd Puck no more we need
   The circuit of the earth to go,
For now, as rapidly as thought,
   From distant climes the news is brought.

We still may burn in mirthful glee
   The nut which truth, nor falsehood tells,
And in the glass we all may see
   Our beau, or lass, without the spells
Which ne'er could give the visage true,
   Daguerre now brings them to our view.

Our Hallowe'en, with mirth, and song,
   With science, literature, and art,
We'll sacred keep,—and may it long
   Remain enshrin'd in every heart;
With all its antiquateds pells,
   Which Burns in song so graphic tells.

Our native land, with every scene,
  We fondly treasure in our minds,
And fondly love our gracious Queen,
  Whose virtues every subject binds;
O, may She long the sceptre wield,
  And God Her realm in mercy shield.

And this, our Fair Adopted Land,
  With rivers, lakes, and mountains vast;
Protected, by Jehovah's hand,
  Her bright'ning prospects long shall last;
While flows her streams, or hills are green,
  We'll ne'er forget our Hallowe'en.

A noble, God-like work is ours,
  To clothe, and feed, the suff'ring poor,
To cheer the widow's lonely hours,
  Saint Andrew's Home to such secure;
With acts like these we ever mean
  Sacred to keep our Hallowe'en.

AN EPITAPH.

Return, dear friends, weep not for me;
  Weep for yourselves, to Jesus flee;
And while you have the means of grace,
  Secure in Christ a hiding place.

THE OLD MAN OF THE QUILL.

The following was written as a dunning article, and was inserted under the editorial heading of a temperance paper, which was the picture of an old man cross-legged, spectacles on eyes, books around him, while the editor himself was only a youth.

The old man of the quill leans back in his chair,
And waits for an idea contentedly there;
For a practical idea, brilliant, and new,
Is of greater value to him, or to you,
Than whole volumes of trash, which comes from the press,
Deriving their value from *titles*, or *dress*.
Cross-legged he sits, and perhaps he's cross-eye'd,—
If he is, the blemish his spectacles hide;
But one thing is quite certain, he sees very straight,
Through Temperance concerns—the Church, and the State.
His books pil'd around him, he doubtless has read,
The contents of which, are all stor'd in his head.
But these are a trifle, to what you would find,
Could you but look in on the shelves of his mind;
There, in order complete, are works old and new,
From Moses quite down to the latest Review.
Yet with knowledge so vast, I "guess," he sometimes
Gets puzzled for ideas, as I do for rhymes.
A wonderful man in this wonderful age,
Must an editor be, to furnish a page,

Which the many shall read, and all, shall admire,
And pay for, as soon, as the "*terms*" shall require.
But weekly, this veteran, sends out a sheet,
So pleasing, so moral, instructive, and neat,
That thousands peruse it, with care, and delight,
And pay in advance for,—OR FAIL TO DO RIGHT.
But some are so careless, or wicked, I fear,
As not to pay up, till the end of the year,
And others, 'tis possible, do not pay then;
But such I should libel, by calling them men.
For look at the picture, and see the old sire,—
His feet nearly frozen for want of a fire,—
His patience, a proverb, how could he endure
So much suff'ring, and toil, if he was not poor?
Come, pay up your bills, and relieve the old gent;
I fear, by his looks, his last dollar is spent.
If human you are, just give proof of it now—
Receive, in return, the old gentleman's bow.
But stop, I've been talking about the old man,
And puzzled my brain, more than puzzle he can,
When I chanc'd, to look up, just over his head,
And there in plain English this sentence I read—
"John F. Coles, Editor,"—I quick dropp'd my pen,
Mistaken alone in the age of the men.

THE EXILE.

He was guilty of rescuing a slave from cruel bondage, and had to flee his country, or suffer in prison, perhaps for years, or a lifetime. He was not pious, but became a Christian from the Providence. O, cursed slavery! Thanks to God, that it has been abolished in the British Empire, the United States, and elsewhere. God grant, it may be soon, very soon, everywhere.

Grief fester'd in his anguish'd heart,
When justice stern bid him depart
From all his friends, and happy home,
An exile o'er the earth to roam.
His grief was follow'd by despair
When home's last hill-top, green and fair,
From distance far with ling'ring look
He view'd, and his last farewell took!
No more, where childhood's hours were spent,
Where at his will, he came, and went;
No more, where youthful sports, and plays,
Gladden'd his heart in bygone days;
No more, where manhood's hopes, and fears,
And changing scenes had mark'd his years,
Shall he, with kindled eye, behold—
No! no! his long adieu is told!

He turn'd away, then look'd again;
Then sank o'erwhelm'd with mental pain:
One prayer he sigh'd—" Death, death, befriend;
Here let this life and anguish end."

'Tis midnight's hour, he still is there,
His hope holds conflict with despair!
The crescent moon, long in its wane,
And twinkling stars, on night's broad plain,
Tho' feeble, their united rays
Were brighter than the noontide's blaze—
Compar'd with hope's expiring flame,
Which flick'ring went, and flick'ring came,
In that sad hour, the chast'ning rod
He felt was in the hand of God!
His sins of childhood, youth, and age,
Before him rose, a darken'd page,—
He view'd, review'd, and ponder'd well
The theme of judgment, heaven, and hell!
Dread Sinai's vivid flash, and peal,
Arous'd his sinful heart to feel;—
He wept, and turn'd to Calvary—
Its Victim was his only plea;
He claim'd, by faith, the atoning blood,
By faith, became a child of God!

His heart still feels, his pulse still beats,
Though long depriv'd of rest, and meats,
O, that that head were pillow'd where
It would not throb with pain, and care.
He cannot now recall the past,
And what he feels must ever last,

While beats his heart, unless some friend,
With kindness, bids that anguish end.

He has no home! no home! no home!
And when will death's kind angel come
To bid his spirit to his God—
To see His smile, or feel His rod?
Years he may live, but shall they be
Such long, dark years of mystery
As those, he last, has sadly known,
With blasted hopes so thickly strewn?
If so, no longer would he live,
But to the deep, dark wave, he'd give
The off'ring of his fading clay,
Nor live to see another day!
But still he hopes, nor will he yield
To dark despair, the doubtful field,
Until again, he effort make
The galling chain to loose, or break.
"Adieu!" he says, "these verses keep,
Remember him, too sad to weep;
They speak the language of a soul
Which only justice can console."

A RIDDLE.

I am confin'd, and yet I'm free
To travel river, land, or sea.
I die to live, and live to die;
While life to others I supply.
I am abus'd by all my friends,
Ground down to dust to serve their ends.
My foes employ my powers to kill,
And make me vile against my will.
Dear children, please to tell my name,
Where I am found, from whence I came.

The Apostle Paul associated my name somewhere with "Thou fool."

A VERSE ON A TOMBSTONE.

While living, never free from danger,
Death must arrest thee, passing stranger!
Pause, then, a moment on this sod,
And here, prepare to meet your God!

A REPROOF.

Stepping one day into a clergyman's study in the basement of his church, and very much exposed, I found his valuable gold pen lying carelessly on his table. I took it up, and wrote the following :—

If Bristol lives a few years more,
He'll see what he ne'er saw before,
And know, what he has never known;
But if he lives, just as he should,
Much will he do for public good,
And not for public good alone.

Those "bumps" above, behind his ear,
Such courage gives, he knows no fear,
But meets, and conquers every foe;
May he be humble, firm, and true,
And do, whatever God says "do,"
While trav'ling through this vale of woe.

I've tried your pen, and find it good;
But had you done, just as you should,
You would not left it lying here,
As a temptation to the weak;
Who might have come, "perchance," to seek
Your prayers, or sympathetic tear.

THE INFIDEL.

Shrouded in darkness, see the man,
Who never reads God's holy Word;
Who never view'd the wond'rous plan
Of bringing rebels back to God.

No love, no joy, no cheering light,
No happiness, no peace of mind,
No hope, no faith, no prospects bright
In all his gloomy path we find.

The ox, the ass, to reason blind,
Discovers full as much as he,
Whose thoughts, words, acts are all combin'd
To oppose God's Word, and plain decree.

The swelling tide of sin's full flood,
Its pain, its sorrow, and remorse,
Oh! How unlike the smile of God,
The easy burden of the Cross.

What pains, forebodings, awful glooms,
The souls who sin are doom'd to feel:
Led like the blind among the tombs,
On ruin's brink, they tott'ring reel,

Without the Saviour, fearful state,
Expos'd to death, eternal death,
They who have sinn'd, until too late
To pray—but curse with latest breath!

O, Saviour! keep my heart from sin,
And lead me on in Wisdom's way,
Till I the crown of life shall win,
And sing Thy praise in endless day.

ON A FRIEND'S MONUMENT.

Here fond affection sheds the tear
O'er him, the husband, father, friend;
Soon other friends shall linger here,
And o'er our graves in sorrow bend.

A WIDOW'S THANKS.

Composed for a widow with four young children,—to give to lady who had supplied her wants.

An angel's hand, an angel's eye,
With pity fill'd, hath hush'd the sigh
  Of a poor widow in distress :—
Whose orphan children are her store—
Two girls, two boys, from twelve to four,
  Without a father's hand to bless.

O kindest, best, of all my friends,
How can I ever make amends
  For all the favors thou hast shown ?
No recompense can I bestow ;
But in my breast I feel a glow,
  Of purest gratitude, alone.

May heavenly joy, and heavenly peace,
Be thine in time, and never cease,
  And may we meet in bliss above,
Where life eternal, shall be given,
To all who do the will of Heaven,
  And as themselves, their neighbors love

"DRINK THE MAD'NING BOWL NO MORE."

"Drink I will, for drink I may,
Late at night or early day,
Brandy, cider, ale, or gin;
Drink I may, 'tis not a sin,
For they are God's creatures good—
Needful as our daily food.

Drink I will, for drink I can,
Yet remain a sober man;
Others may, but I cannot
Ever be a drunken sot!
Prudently I take my cup,
When I breakfast, dine or sup.

"Drink I may, I can, I will,
Precious liquor from the 'still;'
For it drives dull care away,
Turns the darksome night to day;
Makes me noble, rich, and kind;
Wakes my senses, fires my mind.

"Drink I will, for drink I must;
Money gone, I'll drink on 'trust;'
Credit gone, I'll pawn my coat,
Freeze my back to warm my throat!
Stop I cannot, 'tis too late,
Drink I must, or death's my fate!"

"Drink, poor fellow, drink no more,
Hope has opened wide a door,"
Cries the pledg'd cold-water man;
"Surely, if you will, you can
Leave your cups and happy be;
Sign the pledge, and shout, 'I'm free!'"

"Drink again I never will!"
Cries the victim of the "still."
"Stop I can, the pledge I'll sign,
Farewell brandy, cider, wine;
Blind I was, but now I see;
Pledg'd I am, and now I'm free!"

"DRINK THE MAD'NING BOWL NO MORE!"
Let it sound from shore to shore;
Sons and Daughters, old and young,
Let it swell from every tongue;
Washingtonians we'll be,
Bound by that which makes us free!

Let us drink the water cup,
When we breakfast, dine, or sup;
When at marriage feasts we meet,
When long absent friends we greet;
Friendship's token let it be,
Healthful, pleasant, pure and free!

ON THE DEATH OF REV. G. PICKERING.

I've seen thee oft—I see thee still,
As once thou stood'st on Zion's hill,
   A conqu'ring chieftain, firm and bold,
Clad in thy Gospel Armor bright,
To meet the rebel sons of night,
   Stronger than they a thousand fold.

I saw thee oft—I see thee still,
But not upon the battle-hill,
   With helmet, buckler, shield and sword;
For death, thy foe, a friend hath come,
A messenger to call thee home
   To Jesus, thy All-Conqu'ring Lord.

I saw thee oft—I see thee still,
Thy presence comes without the will,
   But choice detains my welcome guest:
I listen to thy notes of praise,
Which lips immortal ever raise
   In thy eternal land of rest.

I see thee now a conqu'ror crown'd,
'Midst hosts of conqu'rors clust'ring round,
   And foremost in that shining crowd,
I see thy compeers here in arms,
With crowns of life, and conqu'ring palms,
   They raise the song of triumph loud.

Wesley and Fletcher press thee near,
Coke, Clark, and Watson too, appear,
   And all the English Wesleyan band
Whom God hath call'd from earth away
To their reward in endless day,
   With those of every age and land.

To see thee Asbury shouts anew,
M'Kendree, George, and Roberts too,
   Whatcoat, and Emory, Fisk, and Lee,
Ostrander, Merritt, all unite
To welcome thee to realms of light—
   Thee, vet'ran, sainted Pick'ring, thee.

I saw thy sacred house of clay
Laid where the living all must lay,
   Until the trump of God shall sound;
Then, rising from its dusty bed,
With Christ, our glorious, risen Head,
   May we, who live, with thee be found.

We saw thee oft, but never more
Shall we behold thee on the shore
   Of time, where still we toil and fight;
But soon the heralds of the Cross,
Who now for Christ count all things loss,
   Shall dwell with thee in realms of light.

THE CARS OF TIME.

The cars roll'd up, then swift away
They haste without a moment's stay;
Too late—and then, with mental pain,
He sees far off the flying train.

How plainly mark'd are all things here
With disappointment, hope, and fear;
But fear, sure founded, gains the day,
And drives all earthly hope away.

But in the humble Christian's soul,
Fear yields to conqu'ring hope's control;
And disappointment finds no place
In him, who trusts God's saving grace.

The Cars of Time, in rapid flight
Move on, as day succeeds to night,
Two cars, two only, form its train—
Salvation one, one Sin and Shame!

Death is the Depot, where we haste,
And waiting there, for all who waste
Their golden moments, stands Despair,
To claim his victims, none to spare!

O leave the car of Shame and Sin;
Step o'er the platform, come, come in,
And run life's track, and glory gain;
Then with our Great Conductor reign.

A HYMN.

Written by request, for the new Hymn Book of the M. E. Church, the publishers having none of this metre in their collection.

Divine Instructor, Lord,
We trust Thy sacred Word,
And ask in faith Thy presence here.
Collected in Thy name,
We now Thy promise claim;
Lord in our midst to bless appear.

Appear, with conqu'ring love,
And all our spirits move
To humble, holy, rapt'rous praise:
For hearts, by grace made pure,
For hopes of heav'n secure,
And all the wonders of Thy grace.

We wait for heav'nly food;
We wait to be renew'd
With strength, which Thou alone canst give,
With faith, and hope, and love,
That, harmless as the dove
And wise as serpents, we may live.

Then shall our lips confess
Thy power divine to bless,
To pardon, and to cleanse from sin;
Many shall see and fear,
And shed contrition's tear,
And run with us the prize to win.

Jesus, the grace impart
To make us pure in heart,
That we may see, and know our God,
And walk the narrow way,
Which leads to endless day,
The holy pathway prophets trod.

We groan to be set free
From sin, and self, to flee
For full redemption in Thy blood.
Thy blood can cleanse from sin,
And make all pure within;
Help, and we plunge the purple flood.

ON A FATHER'S GRAVESTONE.

Call not this spot a place of gloom,
Ah! no, it is my father's tomb.

MAN FROM EDEN WANDERING.

To man from Eden wand'ring,
To man the prey of sin,
While o'er his sorrow pond'ring,
When all was dark within,

The promise of salvation,
In love divine, was given,
Which rais'd to admiration,
His soul in praise to Heaven.

His heart, the seat of sadness,
Is now the seat of joy;
His bosom swell'd with gladness,
Delight without alloy.

The hopes of brighter glory
Now wean his soul from earth;
He loves the Old, Old Story
Of Christ, and the New Birth.

No longer now in sorrow,
He treads the thorny way;
He sees a brighter morrow,
And hails the joyous day.

THE SABBATH SCHOOL.

The Sabbath school, we love it well;
We love it for good reasons;
'Twas there we learn'd the way to heaven,
And had most blessed seasons.

At early morn we rise for prayer,
We thank the Hand that blesses,
We read, and sing, then haste to school,
In our clean Sunday dresses.

Our teachers smile to see us come,
They bid us each good morning;
We say our lessons, then we list
To kind advice, and warning.

We love the school, the Sabbath school,
For there we found a treasure;
It gives us joy to think of it,
The Sabbath school of pleasure.

Let others roam, and waste the day,
They have a night of sadness;
But those who keep God's holy way,
Have nights and days of gladness.

We pity them, who wicked are ;
We hope to see them turning,
To find the blessed Sabbath school,
Where we God's Word are learning.

Come, come, dear children, one and all,
Let's sing and pray together;
And never fail to be at school,
Whatever is the weather.

TO MRS. KEZIA S——R.

God lives above, He sees thy woes,
Thy every thought, word, action knows,
On Him with confidence in prayer,
Cast all your sorrows, pain and care.

Dear sister, raise that drooping head,
Nor let another tear be shed,
For Jesus is your mighty Friend,
Who will be with you to the end—

In safety all thy steps to guide—
O, closely press that Bleeding Side;
Soon all our woes and cares shall cease,
And we with Him shall rest in peace.

CALVARY'S FOUNTAIN.

Where is the balm for every woe,
Where does the healing fountain flow,
To wash away our sinful stains?
Say, does it flow o'er Judah's plains,
Or does it from the altar rise,
Where smokes the bleeding sacrifice?
Or is it Ganges' sacred stream,
Where Asia's sons of glory dream?
No: not through Judah's lowly plain,
Nor from the blood of bullocks slain,
Nor is it Ganges' rolling tide,
But Calvary's stream from Jesus' side.
'Twas open'd by the soldier's spear,
Ah! precious truth the world may hear,
It flows, a world, from sin to save,
To burst the prison of the grave;
Salvation free to all our race;
O! wondrous love, O! boundless grace.
Come to this fountain, sinners come,
Ye halt, and deaf, ye blind and dumb,
Its virtues will your sight restore,
The lame may walk, and halt no more,
The dumb may speak, the deaf may hear,
Come, then, without a doubt or fear.

SLAVERY AND ITS ABOLITION.

PUBLISHED IN 1832.

When, when shall the oppress'd go free?
When shall the sweets of liberty
For Afric's sons be gain'd?—
When all like brethren shall unite,
Red, white, and black, with equal right,
With hearts of love unfeign'd?

Shall it be when the hoarded gold
Of misers, from their coffers told,
Shall freight them o'er the sea?
And colonize them on the shore
Where they, or parents long before,
Were robb'd of liberty?

Or shall we wait for the vast sea
To disappear, and cease to be,
Then drive them from our shore;
Where they have toil'd for many years,
And dress'd the soil with sweat and tears,
Their backs all stain'd with gore?

"Oh, no!" the voice of Wisdom cries;
"Vain hope, to think to colonize
Three million human souls:
As soon expect that Ocean's cup,
By Sol's bright ray, shall be drunk up,
And leave the extended shoals."

"Oh, no!" the voice of Justice cries;
"While dark'ning tempests vail the skies,
And clouds obscure the day;—
Strike! strike! the long suspended blow,
And let the cruel white man know
The madness of his way."

Mercy then cries, "The guilty spare,
The guiltless shall their mercy share,
The black man shall go free;—
Their minds they'll try to elevate,
In reason's scale their talents rate,
And slaves shall cease to be."

O bondage, slavery, worse than death;—
Take liberty, then take my breath,
Take friends, and all possess'd;
But let me keep this boon of Heaven,
Which God to every man hath given,
Without which none are bless'd.

AND IS THERE A GOD?

And is there a God?—dare I,—O fool, that I ask,
For to prove there is none what a laborous task;—
For the power which He gave, such a question to raise,
Fully answers the question, and prompts me to praise
The God of my being, of all beings, and things,
The great Ruler of worlds, of all peoples and kings.
With my heart I adore Him—adoringly fall
At His footstool, so humbly, the vilest of all;
And implore His forgiveness, His mercy, and love,
His protection and aid, that I ever may prove
My allegiance to Him,—His commands all obey
Till He calls me from earth to His presence away.

How blinded our spirit by the god of this world;
Whom pride and rebellion from heav'n's battlements hurl'd,
And who, with fell malice against Almighty Power,
On our race, with dire vengeance, all evil did shower.
Insidious his movements, all forms of disguise;
As an angel of "light," he would dazzle our eyes.
But in "love," thanks to Heav'n, he can never appear,
And when love blends with light, we have nothing to fear.

I rejoice in that Power which the Scriptures unfold,
By which Sin, Death, and Hell, are completely controll'd.
By which man from his weakness, and guilt, may arise
To praise his Creator, in the earth, and the skies.
Emmanuel,—Redeemer,—my Hope, and my Song,
In affliction's fierce furnace,—I'll trust my life long;
For with God to support, I can all things endure,
I need Fountain, and Furnace, to make my heart pure.
All praise to the Father, Holy Spirit, and Son!
The mysterious Godhead—Three Persons in One!
For Creation, Redemption—O wonderous love!
And a heaven of rest in bright mansions above.

TO MY SISTER HANNAH—A WISH.

May ruddy health thy cheeks adorn;
May friends thy path with pleasures strew;
May roses bloom without a thorn;
And peace distil like evening dew.

May hope's bright ray thy future cheer,
And pious deeds thy hours employ;
And every passing day, and year,
Bring with them happiness and joy.

BEARS OR NO BEARS.

In my youth I visited the north-eastern coast of America, and spent a number of months in hunting, fishing, and rambling. One night, after having during the day been blown about twelve leagues from the ship, in a small boat, we made a harbor. The seamen were afraid, if they ventured on shore, that they might be attacked by the bears, which were frequently seen. I therefore gave them permission to remain in the boat, but I preferred the shore, Bears or no Bears. They set me on shore, and then anchored the boat at a safe distance. I clambered up the rugged rocks until I thought myself beyond the reach of the rising tide; and buttoning up my "Pea Jacket," tying down my hat over my ears, and putting on my mittens, I lay down on the sharp stones, and soon fell asleep—not, however, until I had heard the distant growl of Bruin, who, I suppose, would have liked me for his supper.

Dark, gloomy, and chill was that dreary night,
When, on the coast of Labrador,
Without a shelter, food, or light,
I laid me down on the ice-clad shore.

A rock for my pillow, cheerless, and cold,
The broken flints my feathers were,
My heart was like the lion bold,
For near me growl'd the voracious bear.

But there all alone, I rested unharm'd;
With limbs, needing action, I rose,
And though I had slept unalarm'd,
I was stiff from my head to my toes.

And never again may it be my lot,
To suffer such a cheerless night;
I love my home, my humble cot,
My food, bed, fire, and everything right.

Let the red man prize his wild forest home;
And hunt the elk, the deer, and bear;
I'd rather in New England roam,
And share with friends their cot and their fare.

PROPHETIC—1832.

See ye not the morning breaking,
See ye not the day is nigh;
Will ye still with fear be quaking,
Doubt the scripture of the sky?

Of the future, nought more certain,
Slavery from our land shall cease:—
Faith removes the misty curtain
Slavery, War,—then, Freedom,—Peace!

COME, SIGN THE PLEDGE.

The individual whose sentiments I have thrown into verse below, was once within the inner circle of the Maelstrom of intemperance, but is now doing much good as a Temperance Lecturer.

COMPOSED IN 19½ MINUTES.

Dark, sad, and lonely, full of grief,
I wish'd for death to give relief;
   But death came not.
Despair was fast'ning on my soul,
I fled to the accursed bowl,
   And soon forgot

My heart-felt grief,—my mental pain:
But soon, ah! soon I felt again
   With double woe!
And in the madness of despair,
I deeper drank to drown my care,
   And pleasures know.

Thus on I went, from bad to worse,
Till every farthing in my purse
   Was spent for rum!
My watch, my books, my clothes, and trunk,
I sold to keep the drunkard drunk,
   And conscience mum.

Thus years roll'd on, and rum roll'd down
My throat,—the greatest sot in town,
   If not in State;—
And where I soon should sober be,
Was not a doubtful thing to me;
   The grave my fate!

Just then, John Hawkins' voice I heard;
I listened, and my soul was stirr'd;—
   For yet I had
A something in me which could feel
Kind words, express'd in kinder zeal;
   They made me glad.

I signed the pledge, became a man;
And now am doing what I can
   Others to save:
And have no doubt but scores can say
I've lov'd them from their cups away,
   And from the grave!

Come then, dear fellows, stop and think;—
Resolve you will no longer drink
   The hateful stuff!
Come, sign the PLEDGE, and happy be,
From rum, wine, beer, and cider, free,
   With cash enough

Yes, sign the pledge, and soon you'll find
Old friends will rally round you kind;—
    And many new
Will cheer your heart with right good will;
Friendship and love your cup shall fill
    With pleasures true.

"LOOK NOT ON THE DARK SIDE."
AN ACROSTIC.

Look not on the dark side until you grow cold,
Yet look on the dark side, with faith, and grow bold.
Mark well the dark features, and dwell on the light,
Assur'd by the promise, not walking by sight.
Not trusting in man, but alone in your God,
Contend for the pathway your Saviour once trod,
Use none but the weapons of kindness and love,
Taking Christ for your pattern, with strength from above.
Leave nothing undone 'tis your duty to do,
Endeavor with patience your way to pursue,
Rising higher in grace, till glory you view.

POETIC CARD.

Said Bunyan,—
"I knew a man—some people called him mad—
The more he gave away the more he had;"
Such men in N—— still are living,
They're getting rich, and always giving.

As bees to hive with precious store,
So swarms of friends approach'd our door;
They loaded came, from every part
Of N—— all with cheerful heart,
And left their loads, that we might share
In things to eat, and drink, and wear.
As bees bring wax, and then the honey,
So they brought goods, and then the money.
But list awhile, and hear the sequel.
Of goods they brought in value equal
To dollars Fifty-Three, or Four;
In cash as much, and little more,—
Making ONE HUNDRED EIGHT in all
They left in their "Donation Call,"
For which our grateful thanks we give;
Long may such kindly donors live
To bless mankind by their example,
Of deed so noble, broad, and ample.
A blessing on them,—" Friends indeed,"—
May Heaven supply their every need;
And when life's busy scenes are o'er,
May we all reach the heavenly shore,
And there the People and the Pastor
Be jewels of our Lord and Master.

THE CALIFORNIAN CRY.
AN IRONICAL POEM.

Away to California, boys!
  Sounds loud from every quarter;
Away to California, boys!
  By over-land or water.
Away! regardless of the tears
  Of mother, wife, or daughter!
Away, away! without delay,—
  It will not do to loiter!

To San Francisco, haste! O haste!
  The oracles are saying;
For near that place, o'er hill and dale,
  The gold, in lumps, is laying!
Then linger not—a fortune's lost,
  For every hour's delaying;
But haste away! for nothing stay!
  For all is lost by staying.

Away! the Sacramento's wave
  O'er mines of gold is rolling;
Let not affection's hand detain,—
  Don't stop with friends condoling!

To wife and sweetheart bid adieu,
    And check the tear that's strolling
Adown the cheek,—and haste away!
    For gold is all-consoling!

Away! for Madam Fortune's tide,
    In your affairs is flowing;
Away to California, then!
    Where she is now bestowing
With open hand, alike to all,
    Who'll catch it while 'tis going;—
Then do not stay, for fear she may
    Her fickle mind be showing!

Away! from the Green Mountains' slopes,
    To mountains bright and yellow!
Away! from barren Granite hills,
    Where cattle roam and bellow,—
From fields where corn and pumpkins grew,
    On soil once rich and mellow!
Away, away! for if you stay,
    You are a stupid fellow!

From Maine and Massachusetts start,—
    From every street and alley!
Let all New England hear the call,
    And all New England rally!

Leave plough and workshop—haste away!
  To the enchanted valley!
Away, away! and sport and play
  With millions, without tally.

Away, away! from South and West—
  Both married men and single!
Let black, and white, and brown, and red,
  In one vast body mingle!
Let masters shout, "Ye slaves, be free!"
  Then many ears shall tingle,—
And hosts, with song, shall rush along,
  From every hill and dingle!

Away! whose god is Mammon,—
  From State or Territory—
And bow and worship at his shrine,—
  Youth, middle-ag'd, and hoary.
Let none refuse to bend the knee—
  Whig, Democrat, or Tory;
Haste; haste, I say! your homage pay—
  And give to him the glory!

Away to California, then,
  The place of Mammon's choosing;
Away to Sacramento's stream,—
  Your chances don't be losing.

By sail and steam, your way pursue,
    Nor stop a moment musing:
Away, away! by night and day,
    Both wind and tide be using.

Away, away! from classic halls,
    An idle thing is learning;
Go turn the leaves of virgin gold,—
    They'll pay you well for turning.
Yes; haste! begone! while youthful fires
    In youthful veins are burning;
Away, away! and show to-day
    You truly are discerning.

Shut down the gates; shut off the steam,—
    No further need of spinning
The thread of cotton, flax, or wool,
    But gold of your own winning.
And warp and woof of shining stuff,
    We'll wear, instead of linen.
Then haste away, nor lose a day,
    To linger would be sinning.

The Doctor there may fill his purse,
    Without his neighbors' dying;
The Lawyer, too, may wealthy grow,
    And cease forever lying.

And Ministers, in worldly pelf
  May with them both be vying.
Then haste away, for sure you may
  Move slow enough by flying.

Around the Horn—a pleasant voyage—
  We'll sail in ships so cheerly;
Or else by Gulf and Isthmus route—
  A pleasant journey, merely—
To that delightful promise-land,
  Where all is gold—or nearly.
Then, haste away; why will you stay,
  Where starve you must, most clearly?

But I must haste, and end my song—
  If I can find an ending,
Amidst a crowd of useful thought,
  All to your welfare tending.
Once more I say, awake! awake!
  And on your way be wending;
Haste! haste away! or soon the day
  Will come to you heart-rending.

But here I end, for end I must—
  Our topsails loos'd for sailing,—
Our colors floating—to the mast
  The crew have just been nailing;

And soon far off, upon the sea,
  We'll leave you, out of hailing;
Then once for all, I sound the call—
  O, may it prove availing.

ADVERTISEMENT.

As my book is entitled "Variety," I give the following advertisement, which was published in one of the largest cities of the U. S. for a year in a daily paper. The Merchant for whom I wrote it had been slandered by reports that he was about "failing," "selling out," or "assigning;" hence the allusion in the first line.

Not dead, not sold, nor yet assign'd;
Midst wooden ware Colburn you'll find,
At my old stand in Osborn's block,
Free as a bird, firm as a rock,
Ready to wait on one, and all
Who please to make a business call.
You'll find my stock is large and good,
Whether of silver, gold, or wood;
Here's brooms and brushes, pails and tubs—
Cradles on wheels with shining hubs:
Baskets of every form and size,
For every use you can devise;
Chairs for the young, chairs for the old—
Ice tanks, to keep your water cold;

Cages for birds, and traps for mice;
Spitoons to keep your carpets nice;
Wash-boards, mop-handles, and clothes frames,
And everything the housewife names
Or needs, from attic to the cellar
You'll find at " COLBURN'S "—" *Curious Fellar !*"
Here's fancy goods, and pleasing toys,
For ladies, gents, their girls and boys,
Of German, French, and Chinese make—
To name them all a quire 'twould take;
Guitars and fiddles, fifes and drums
For men and boys, when Christmas comes;
Here's silver, gold, and plated ware;
Knives, forks, and spoons of finish rare;
Breast-pins and fobs, and chains and rings,
Keys, clasps, and jet and coral strings,
And things by thousands yet untold
Of wood, of silver, steel, and gold.
Wholesale or retail, come and buy,
So cheap, you nowhere else will try:
But one thing more, and then I'm done,
My number is one hundred one.

PROSE

BY THE

BARD OF NIAGARA.

My first born died in her tender moments. My second and third daughters, I had the pleasure, by my Sacred office, to unite in holy wedlock.

My fourth daughter was married by another, while I was absent far from home, and the following "paper," which I had sent them, was read on the occasion. My fifth, *a son*, died in early childhood.

FIVE BUDS IT BORE.

Five buds it bore, but three of them only bloomed; and all of them now are plucked from the parent Stalk. The first, while yet a tender bud, the King chose to deck His Son's triumphant brow.

The next, full blown, a passing stranger saw, and asked the Gardener for. The Gardener smiled assent; the flower was plucked.

The third, a rose in bloom, another stranger saw and wished, and asked for. Again the Gardener smiled, and bade him pluck the flower.

Another bloom there was, the last upon the Stalk; for so well the first had pleased the King, He sent His messenger and took the other opening bud so beautiful, for the same purpose that he took the first. And now but one, fair as the fairest of them all, remained. But while a season absent from His garden, a stranger plucked that bloom without the Gardener's leave.* The Gardener sighed, but was content; for so well He loved the stranger, He had smiled again, and gave the flower if asked.

The Stalk still lives, no less beautiful, though robbed of buds and flowers.

The Gardener prized those buds so beautiful and flowers so fair. The Stalk He prizes more, and wishes life protracted no longer than it lives!

MONTREAL, 1853.

* He had asked by letter, but the letter miscarried.

AN ESSAY

ON THE QUESTION—IS THE DIVISION OF CHRISTIANS
INTO SECTS AN EVIL?

DELIVERED BEFORE THE YOUNG MEN'S ASSOCIATION OF ST. JAMES
STREET WESLEYAN METHODIST CHURCH, 1871.

This is a question of moment, and one which should be duly considered, and candidly answered.

If it can in truth be answered in the affirmative, such an answer should be rendered, and the arguments to support the same adduced, that all who have embraced the opposite opinion may be convinced of their error.

If, on the contrary, we find arguments clear and cogent to sustain the negative, it is of no small importance that they be advanced, that the tongue of bigotry and the cavilings of the sceptic be silenced, and that Infidelity be deprived of one of its most powerful weapons of assault on the Christian Church.

The question, I apprehend, does not include all who call themselves Christians irrespective of doctrines which they may hold as fundamental, though diametrically opposed to the " Faith once delivered to the saints; " but those only who admit the great doctrines of the Bible, and are contending, as best they may, for those foundation principles on which they are building their hopes of heaven.

If the question should be construed so as to embrace the numerous semi-Christian, or perhaps more properly semi-Infidel sects of this and past periods of the Christian era, I should without hesitation submit an affirmative answer.

Another question, having a bearing on the subject, it will be well to settle before we proceed to the discussion, viz. Are we to understand the main question to refer to division in itself, and legitimate effects alone considered, or in connection with the many abuses and illegitimate consequences of division which to all are apparent?

Many things, we know, which are in themselves good, are by abuse made subservient to evil.

Fire in itself is a good, and when properly and carefully used, its effects are good; but when not thus used, it is an evil.

Knowledge, too, when properly used, is a good; yet how deplorable are its effects when made subservient to the accomplishment of evil.

The division of Christians into sects may in itself be a good, notwithstanding evils may be traced back to it as their source.

We are to judge of things by their effects to determine whether they are good or evil; but it must be from natural, legitimate, and uniform effects, if we would have our conclusion drawn in truth.

Understanding, then, the question to include those only who admit the fundamental doctrines of the Bible, and who differ only in points of minor importance, and in the externals of the Christian system, such as forms of Government, Rites, and Ceremonies; and also that the abuses and illegitimate effects of division are not referred to in the question, we proceed to its discussion.

Is, then, "THE DIVISION OF CHRISTIANS INTO SECTS AN EVIL?" We answer, No; and assert that, so far from being an evil it is a good, and is attended with benefits to the Church and the world.

THE FIRST REASON we offer in support of this assertion is—

That the division of Christians into sects affords collateral evidence that the System of Christianity is of divine origin.

Had Christianity been of human origin, and its votaries divided, as they now are, into sects—holding as they do many conflicting sentiments, and having distinct forms of ecclesiastical government and disciplinary regulations;— instead of a present flourishing existence, it would have long since shared the fate of other human schemes!

Where shall we look for any system of man's device, which has for any considerable period remained unchanged and unbroken, supported by sects as widely differing in opinions as the sects composing the Christian body? We look for them in vain.

But, on the contrary, we do find lamentable proofs of the destructibility of the best wrought systems of men—systems which have dazzled in their morning splendor but to make the decreasing light of their short day of glory the more apparent; the night of their extinction having been hastened on by the discordant opinions of their votaries.

Not so with the Christian System. For more than eighteen hundred years it has stood firm, though its members have been, and now are, divided into sects, each of which has zealously defended its distinctive differences, and oftentimes too with a zeal unwarranted by justice or by reason. Proof this, then, that the mystery of its perpetuity is the Divinity of its origin.

And is not any argument which assists to sustain this point a benefit rather than an evil?

THE SECOND REASON we offer as a proof of the assertion is—

That, by the jealous watchfulness of the different sects of Christians, the Holy Scriptures have been handed down to us in their original purity.

We cannot for a moment doubt, after the attempts which have been made in our own day, and in former periods, to pervert the Word of God, that the original text would have been perverted to accommodate the ever-changing opinions of depraved minds, so that it would not be what it now is—the only infallible rule of faith and practice—had it not been for the plurality of Christian sects.

How unsuccessful would be the attempt to change any portion of the Book of Life, so as to introduce any new precept, or expunge any originally there.

Checked by the ever-watchful eye of interested sects, no one has ever succeeded in the attempt; and all who have attempted, have been held up to the execration of an indignant Church.

How have the Christian sects been recently aroused by the affrontive act of certain sectaries, who have only substituted a term of limited import to define the mode of administering a Christian sacrament for one which leaves the mode undefined?

If, then, there is a united expression of disapprobation to this act, and protestation against it, what would have been the feeling if, instead of changing a term, to define a mode of administering a rite, they should have changed terms, so as to have abrogated or changed the rite itself?

While, then, the Church is blest with a division of her body into sects, we may expect the Oracles of Truth to remain unaltered and uncorrupted ; but when no longer guarded by sectarian vigilance, they may be perverted by designing, depraved minds, and cease to be what they now are, the only infallible guide over the stormy sea of life to the haven of eternal rest.

OUR THIRD REASON for our assertion is that

The influence Christian sects exert on each other is to kindle and keep alive the spirit of holy emulation in the Church.

There is in the human mind a tendency to inactivity especially in the performance of good acts.

This tendency is to be found in the regenerated, as well as in the unregenerated mind; hence the necessity of such Scripture exhortations as, " Be diligent in business, fervent in spirit ;" " Let us not be weary in well doing," &c.

When, for any considerable period, a sect of Christians have been isolated from the stimulating influences of other sects, they have often relapsed into a state of spiritual supineness ; the fire of their devotions has burned with a diminished flame, and, in too many instances, has ceased to burn at all.

Many painful illustrations of this fact are to be found chronicled on the pages of Church history.

Though too little Christian zeal is exhibited where many sects are found, yet there is not that deathlike formality, that almost entire conformity to the world, which is too often the case where there is not a plurality of Christian denominations.

The religious history of New England affords an example, though less striking than many, yet the lines of which are traced sufficiently deep to impress on the mind the dark picture of a lukewarm Church.

Though there is much, very much, to deplore in our present history in the want of spirituality, yet less deplorable by far than when a Whitfield, a Lee, and others first visited this land.

By considering one another as sects, we provoke unto love and good works, stirring up each other's pure minds by way of remembrance of duty, endeavoring to excel each other in the God-like work of saving souls.

Where a number of Christian sects exist, there is a kind of holy moral friction which is not only the means of developing the latent fire of Christian enterprise, but which removes also the accumulated rust of Christian inactivity, and burnishes and brightens the chain of Christian fellowship and union.

When the Christian bodies shall have their rays of influence concentrated by the lens of love, Infidelity, Slavery and Intemperance, with their kindred evils, shall melt away under its focal power; the impurities of misnamed Christianity by it shall be removed, and the gold, free from the alloy of error, shall be of standard weight in the scales of the sanctuary.

But when thus concentrated for power, like the rays of light they lose not their distinctiveness, for the prism of truth refracts, and reason reflects them again, in all their primary beauty, and simple moral loveliness.

Questions of vast importance to the well-being of man, in time and in eternity, are now to some good extent enlisting the energies of the Christian world. The great battle of principle is to be fought. The enemy is in the field, under the standard of the Prince of Darkness; and with the desperation of despair, they furiously press on to destroy.

But the spirit of holy rivalship, we doubt not, will soon bring the united force of the Sacramental hosts into the field to oppose them. Each division, led on by their own officers; disciplined by their own laws; marshalled under their own banners; their weapons, of heavenly temper, from one armory; their stores from one magazine; and they obeying the command of one General Officer—whose conquering name is on His thigh, the King of kings, and the Lord of lords; looking upon their several banners and seeing their mottos—" Free grace," " Partial election," " Immersion the only Christian Baptism," &c., and each believing their motto to be divine; and wishing to exhibit to all the effects of its divinity, they will press with greater vigor and courage to the conflict, signalizing themselves by deeds of noble daring not to be excelled by others whose creeds, in their opinion, are less divine and whose discipline is less scriptural. In their holy ardor they will not be checked by the taunts of their fiend-like enemies, as they exclaim, " A sectarian thing;" for over their several banners will float the blood-stained banner of Prince Emmanuel, bearing the initial motto " I. H. S.," followed by the words, " One in Christ Jesus," and, " God forbid we should glory, save in the cross of Christ," but with all the courage which faith and hope imparts, they will meet their hostile foe.

What power shall be able to cope with this?

One of these divisions shall chase a thousand; and two, with their combined power, shall put ten thousand to flight; and when all are thus united and in the field, they will rout the hosts of darknes *en masse*, and earth will bow and yield allegiance to Him whose right it is to reign from the river to the ends of the earth. Yes, when there need be no curse on "Meroz, for not coming up to the help of the Lord against the mighty," Christ's kingdom shall become a universal kingdom, and the Babel language of semi-infidel sects shall be lost in the pure dialect of Canaan, now spoken by the evangelical tribes of modern Israel. Heaven speed on the glorious day of triumph!

THE FOURTH REASON we offer is—

That the division of Christians into sects is a source of harmony to the Church.

This may appear at first sight a strange assertion, but though strange, yet, nevertheless, we believe it to be true. When we reflect on the vast number of minds of different make, and the great variety of subjects for those minds to decide upon, we wonder that there are so few differences of opinion and so great a degree of union among us, rather than that we differ at all, and are not perfectly united. The doctrines of Christ, so plainly set forth by the Evangelists and Apostles, afford but little ground for a diversity of views.

But in the Government, Forms, and Rites less plainly taught, if taught at all, are found fruitful scources for opinions as diverse from each other as are really existing among us. Had Christ as clearly taught that the Presbyterian form of government was the only form for His Church, as He taught the doctrine of salvation by faith, it would, we aver, have been as readily received by Christians. But nowhere does He point us to any specific code of ecclesiastical law, or system of Church government, but leaves the whole subject open.

And for what purpose, we ask, is the subject thus left open? May we not safely answer, and without fear of successful contradiction, to the intent that His followers might introduce any form which they in sober reason might choose; provided, that no form adopted should authorise any individual or individuals "to lord it over God's heritage."

If, then, the Church had selected the form of Government named above to the exclusion of the Episcopal and Independent forms, is it reasonable to suppose, that there would have been found as many satisfied minds as are now to be found within the pale of the Christian Church?

Who, we ask, in the absence of direct command, has a right to say what form shall, or shall not, be adopted, by beings who lose not their free moral agency, and power of volition, by becoming Christians?

Unless, then, it can be shown, that Christians had no right to choose, and also that it would have been better that no system of government should have been adopted, and that the Church should have been ungoverned, contrary to the principle "That any form of government is better than no government," it will follow consequently that individual Christians had a right to choose any form of government not derogatory to Christianity, the elements of which being found in the Book of Equity, Justice, and Truth, under which they might secure the approbation of Heaven, and be made a blessing to a perishing world.

If, then, we have a right to choose in reference to forms of Church government, have we not, under the same "Perfect law of liberty," a right to worship the God of our fathers under our own vine and fig tree, according to the dictates of a Spirit-enlightened conscience, and to choose in other and all matters relating to the Church, in the absence of divine command and prohibition?

The mode of administering Christian baptism we conceive to have been left undefined, for the same reason that no plan of Church government was specified by the Saviour. And not only the mode, but also who are, and who are not, in every instance proper candidates for this ordinance.

And whose *ipse dixit*, we ask, shall be law in the premises?

There are also many doctrines which, in a comparative sense, are called minor, some of which are not so plainly taught as the fundamental doctrines; and others are constructively drawn from the words of Christ and His Apostles, in which we may, and we think do, honestly and sincerely differ, and if we thus differ, do we not differ innocently?

If, then, all sects were to be merged in one with the existing grounds for a diversity of conflicting opinions, would there not be intestine broil and continued discord, instead of the increased and increasing harmony which now obtains in our modern Israel?

Every intelligent and rational Christian may find among the many sects, one with which he can unite in doctrine, discipline, and general usage, so nearly, as to secure the most cordial fellowship. This union, being voluntary, will be the more firm and lasting, and untrammeled; and, free in his own volitions, he is the better prepared to admit and defend the rights of others, and the spirit of religious toleration and enlarged Christian benevolence would drive the spirit of cruel and hateful bigotry far beyond the pale of the Church, even to its native region below.

Charles the Fifth, Emperor of Germany, after the failure of a skilful artisan in his employ so to perfect the mechanism of a number of clocks as to secure their striking alike, arrived at the conclusion that if clocks could not be made to strike alike, it was folly to attempt to make men think alike.

Happy would it have been for tens of thousands, whose blood flowed in consequence of his zeal to maintain the doctrine that a plurality of sects was an evil, if this experiment had been made by him in early, instead of advanced life.

Well would it have been for the Church of God in every period of her history, had her leading minds arrived at the same wise conclusion, and had adopted the sentiment " To think, and let think." Her history's page would not then have been polluted with records of blood, ay, the blood of millions, whose only crime was that of using the boon of Heaven—the "Freedom of Thought!"

Had this sentiment prevailed in the English Church, the famous or rather infamous Act of Conformity in the 16th century—which drove from her communion hundreds of her most pious ministers and tens of thousands of her living members—would not have been even entertained as debatable, instead of becoming a law of the realm under the auspicious Elizabeth.

If, then, there is a variety of important subjects connected with the Christian system which are not plainly defined in the Word of God; if harmony in a great degree depends on the sameness of opinions of individuals composing an organized body; and if men cannot be made to think alike, may we not, must we not, come to the conclusion—" Truth being stranger then fiction "—that Harmony may be, and is promoted by Division?

Our fifth reason for supporting the negative of this question is—

That the controversies which have been the result of conflicting opinions of Christian sects, have led to a more critical perusal of the Bible, and to a clearer development of its truths.

The great controversies which have enlisted the rarest talents of the Church, for the few centuries past, have been the means of eliciting truths of no minor importance to Christian theology, and of scattering those truths broadcast throughout the Christian world.

Giant minds have explored the magazine of truth, and brought forth from thence stores of thoughts that breathe and truths that burn, which would have remained hidden and inoperative had a Calvin and an Armenius never promulgated their conflicting theological sentiments to the world.

How many have been induced, Berean-like, " To search the Scriptures, to see if these things be so?" and, by so doing, have dug deep in the mine of Inspiration; and following the rich veins of truth, have found priceless treasures to repay them for their toil. Instead of lying unused until the language in which they were written had become obsolete, how many copies of God's Book have been literally worn out by individuals who had become biblical students in consequence of controversies which have grown out of questions relating to Scripture doctrines, and the administration of Gospel ordinances?

In wearing out those volumes, deep prejudices against the truth, have been worn away by the truth, and deep stains of moral pollution have been washed out in the cleansing fountain of the Blood of Atonement, to which they have been directed by the Sacred Page they had so critically examined.

Have not the polemic writings of a sainted Fletcher, called forth by the sectarian pen of a Toplady, prompted many to the close investigation of the Oracles of Life, the result of which has been the expansion of mind, the purification of spirit, and the lighting up the pathway of thousands to endless bliss.

To be sure, controversies like these are not without their evils, but it should be remembered that their evils are transient, while their benefits are permanent. The fire of polemic strife is like that of the smitten steel, while the truths elicited by controversy, like fires on Jewish altars, ever burn.

OUR LAST REASON for a negative answer to this question is—

That though thus divided, God smiles upon, and blesses the Church.

In taking an enlarged view of the good which has been and is now being done, through the instrumentality of the Church, do we not involuntarily exclaim, " What has God wrought ?"

If we look at the wonders of His grace, as displayed in the conversion of happy millions, many of whom are now in glory, by our own Church as the agent, and in the same period the millions through the sanctified instrumentalities of other branches of the Christian family, can we come to a conclusion so preposterous as this, that God would approbate that which is in itself an evil, and make it the honored instrument of so much good to our fallen world?

If the division of Christians into sects is an evil, we may not with the Apostle inquire, "Shall we do evil that good may come?" for the question is settled, and we may with confidence and success continue in our evil way, blessing and being blest.

And if evil of some magnitude is smiled upon by Heaven, may we not add evils of greater magnitude, and expect the greater blessing?

We must, then, without continuing farther in thought connected with the argument. conclude that the God of holiness places His seal of approbation on an evil, or that the negative is the only tenable answer to the question.

Let us inquire, then, as we recapitulate the reasons offered.

If the division of Christians into sects affords an argument to prove the system to be divine; if, by the watchfulness of sects, the Bible is preserved in its original purity; if divisions tend to kindle and keep alive the spirit of devotion and religious zeal; if errors have been exposed and truths elicited by controversies which have grown out of conflicting theological sentiments; if a plurality of sects tends to promote harmony in the Church; and if God smiles upon and blesses the Church thus divided, must we not either do violence to our understanding, or admit that the negative is proved, and the assertion sustained?

Let us, then, understandingly pray that Christians may be one in spirit in Christ Jesus, though thus divided into sects: that we may be bound together with cords of love, and be made superior to the combined force of the uncircumcised in heart, leagued with the powers of darkness: that led on by our spiritual Joshua by Him, and with Him take the possession promised—"*Ask* of me and I shall give thee the heathen for thine inheritance, and the uttermost parts of the earth for thy possession:" and that, though thus divided, we may, by the projectile force of Divine Command, the centrifugal power of Free Moral Agency, balanced by the centripetal power of Supreme love to God, revolve on in our orbits of duty, within the Zodiac of Truth, around the Sun of Righteousness, enlightened, and beautified by His effulgent, life-giving, and soul-cheering rays of grace divine, reflecting those rays on each other, to the glory of "Him Who is the Father of lights, with Whom there is no variableness, neither shadow of turning."

A CRITICISM,

By the Bard of Niagara, the appointed critic on a discussion of the question, "Which is best adapted to develop character—Poverty or Riches?" by the Young Men's Association of the Great St. James Street Wesleyan Methodist Church, January 5th, 1872.

Mr. PRESIDENT,—LADIES AND GENTLEMEN,—I cannot accuse myself of ingratitude when I say to you candidly, that I come before you this evening without one word of thanks for the position in which you have placed me by appointing me the critic of the "discussion" on the evening of our last gathering here.

I had much rather be the subject of criticism, than to criticise. And I hope you will not be sparing in honest and truthful criticism on my production this evening, with one exception, viz., That of my pronunciation. Once I **was young, now I am old**, a specimen of dilapidated humanity. I am not in possession of a particle of the dental machine which you all know is so important in distinct articulation; and when I speak in public, I am very careful to select words to convey my thoughts, which I can to some good extent master in their pronunciation.

Not so, however, when I write; and I fear that I have introduced some words into this paper, which I shall be under the necessity of skipping, when I arrive at the point where they should be uttered.

I feel it, Sir, a duty when a work is assigned to me to perform —by those who have a right to assign—to perform that work as best I may, however repugnant to my feelings.

I am impressed, Sir, with the thought that the duty allotted to me this evening ought not to commence with the discussion of the last evening, but rather with the individual or individuals who framed and presented the question discussed.

Is it not a dubious question? And if the principle of Roman jurisprudence be correct—"Lex dubia non obligat"—it would follow that, as the question comes under the head of "Dubia," the parties to whom the question was assigned for discussion were under no binding obligation to discuss it; and if they attempted its discussion, were not subjects of blame if they failed to arrive at a lucid and definite conclusion.

Which is best adapted to develop Character—Poverty or Riches?

What character, we ask? For is it not plainly to be seen, and I hesitate not to assert it is self-evident, that Riches is absolutely and indispensably necessary to develop some of the numerous characters we could name. For instance, a Legal, a Clerical, or Medical? What books, what apparatus, what time, which is said to be money, is absolutely necessary to develop their several characters at the Bar, in the Pulpit, and in the Sickroom?

A Political character may be developed by a poor man who is blessed with common sense and has lived in society. Not so, however, with a Literary, a Military, or a Nautical character, and many others. To bring these out, money, time, and practice are needful, and without these they must remain undeveloped.

Which of these named does the question allude to? Or does it allude to all, or to neither? I may be mistaken, Sir; but from the general drift of the discussion, I was led to the conclusion that the discussers supposed the question referred to a Moral character, or to a Religious, which cannot exist independently of the former; and that it was this character the proposer intended. If so, why did he not use the qualifying term, and have given a definite object to sustain, or oppose, instead of universal terms, which open a field of investigation so boundless?

With the question thus defined, the disputants would not have been in danger of combating their own principles with which they commenced, ere they had concluded their remarks.

Again, the question is dubious, from the fact that there is no line of demarkation drawn between Riches and Poverty.

It must be recollected that these terms are relative and often provincial in their character. What has been esteemed riches in one clime, state and age, frequently has been considered of no value in another clime, state, and age. How many full cargoes of the Great Eastern would it take, of the article which the aboriginal inhabitants of this continent regarded as Riches, to constitute either of us wealthy? The more we had, Sir, of "Wampum," especially if we had to provide storage, the poorer we should consider ourselves to be.

See that man on the Labrador coast (I have seen him) surrounded by hundreds in squalid want, who were looking up to him as the most wealthy man in the to them known world. But in what did his great wealth consist? Had he a magnificent mansion? His costly equipage of fine horses and carriages, and servants in livery? His extensive parks, with their serpentine walks and macadamised driveways? His artificial lakes and unnatural cascades? Verily not. Nor had he hoarded Gold, or Bank or Railroad Stocks, but he did have an old ill-shaped, unpainted, badly rigged, leaky, crazy craft, of about 30 tons burden, and a small framed house without a single feature of the Ionic, Tuscan, Corinthian, Doric, or Composite orders of architecture; but yet he was rich, Vastly rich!

The best conditioned individual present, in regard to wealth, would be considered poor in a neighborhood of Rothschilds, Barings, Astors, and Vanderbilts.

Locke says,—"Riches do not consist in having much gold and silver, but in having more than our neighbor!"

As, then, the question is stated without any qualification, or explanation of what, and in what, Riches and Poverty consist, are we not, and were not the disputants, at a loss to select individuals, who have appeared on the wide arena of human history, as proper subjects to illustrate either position?

But, Mr. President, I suppose that you, Sir, with the ladies and gentlemen before me, by this time are inquiring, if what I have already said is the porch to my house, of what dimensions must the house be if in symmetrical proportion? and you may be fancying a temple as large as Diana's at Ephesus. But I have not studied proportion in my building.

THE GENTLEMAN who opened the discussion in favor of Poverty being the best developer of character, did so with arguments well stated, and illustrations as apt and pertinent, with few exceptions, as are to be found. Had a Homer, a Milton, a Scott, and others named, been, as he asserted, poor, his illustrative arguments would have been more conclusive, but minus proof, they in a degree lost their power to convince us that the position he had taken was tenable.

That of the Prodigal Son could, with nearly the same propriety, have been used for or against his position. For did not Riches as well as Poverty act on his moral and intellectual constitution, resulting in the character of a penitent?—Riches, profligacy and sensuality; Poverty, degradation and want combined, in a result, not of developing a character innate, but a new character, ornated with moral virtues and Christian graces?

The assertion of the Redeemer, that "It is easier for a camel to go through the eye of a needle than for a rich man to enter into the kingdom of God," at first thought appeared a strong argument on the side of Poverty. But when the assertion is examined, we find it was not *riches* but the *trust* in uncertain *riches*. It is not money which is the root of all evil, as was misquoted by one of the disputants, but the love of money. And, so far as we know to the contrary, the poor love money as much, or it may be, even more, than the rich. So far from being true that money is the root of all evil, we assert it is the root of much good. In what state would our Benevolent and Religious enterprizes be without it? The illustrations show that some were poor and pious, not that Poverty developed piety.

The spirit of this speaker appeared kind and courteous, and he showed by his manner and matter that he was governed by a principle to discover truth, rather than dogmatically to sustain an error.

THE SECOND DISPUTANT evinced a spirit of candor, and with some warmth advanced his arguments in favor of Riches being the better developer of character. The individuals he named as illustrative of his position might or might not have been rich. Daniel and his pious coadjutors, though men of distinction, were captive Jews, and as such, had been deprived of their wealth: the inference therefore is that they were poor. Nehemiah with more probability had some wealth, though a captive, and if so, was a good argument to sustain the assertion. The Elector of Saxony—was it his riches or his position which enabled him to act so noble a part in the protection and defence of Luther, who was shaking Europe to its circumference and Rome to its centre? He had wealth as an auxiliary, to be sure, but what effect had that wealth on his character? Might he not have developed the same had he been poor?

Watt, Davey, Clive, Havelock, Pitt, Wellington, and others, which the speaker presented, each and all, depended more on favorable circumstances than on riches, for the accomplishment of their many praiseworthy and noble acts.

Dr. Coke, I ween, in all probability would have been a Dr. Coke with or without riches.

THE THIRD DISPUTANT, at his opening, made a good advance towards giving some clearness to the question, and for a few moments gave promise of bringing it out in its true aspect; but soon a mist came over the scene, and his lucidity suffered an eclipse. He succeeded so far as to bring to our view a good and a bad character; but did he succeed to show that it was Riches that made Napoleon what he was, and as he asserted, continued to be?

Jeffery too,—that foulest blot on England's legal escutcheon—did the disputant make it plain to us that it was Riches in any sense which developed the Neronic Devil-like character, which he exhibited for a long period as Lord Chief Justice, or rather Chief Injustice of the Court of King's Bench?

And were not the same elements in operation to produce that star of the first magnitude, that glory of English jurisprudence who filled the same office,—Sir Matthew Hale—a Lord Chief Justice indeed!

This speaker brought before us the Rich Man and Lazarus, which was as pertinent and convincing as any argument *pro* or *con* in the discussion. I was somewhat surprised, Sir, that no one of the disputants introduced the young man of riches, who went to the Redeemer with that all important question which, when answered by lips Divine, caused him to go away sorrowful. This, if any, would have been an argument to the point.

This speaker's misquotation of Scripture was one of too frequent occurrence in, and out of the pulpit, making a *thing* the root of all evil, instead of the *love* of a thing, as the text unmarred asserts.

It was to be regretted this speaker had not had time to repare himself for the discussion. His forcible style and energetic manner, with other qualifications, give promise that he may yet become a debater of no mean capacity.

THE FOURTH GENTLEMAN'S remarks were short, comprehensive, and pithy; but followed in the same train without any clearly and well defined point at which to aim his active and somewhat forcible blows. His argument expressed in connection with the infamous "New York Ring," I do not think was appreciated according to its merit. It served, however, the purpose of moving some of the muscles of the face which are usually put into requisition to produce a cheerful countenance. He, too, possesses talent which Poverty or Riches, or both, if they truly are developers, should develop.

THE FIFTH SPEAKER took the ground that Poverty was the great agent to cause the seeds of character to germinate, flower, and fruit. He opened with a spirit which seemed to say, "I believe what I assert;" a spirit, Sir, we all should cultivate, if we would excel in our attempts to convince others that what we say is not only Law but Gospel too.

His Goldsmith, with his natural distaste for labor, except when at his meals, and his other illustrations, were more amusing than convincing, but had a pleasing effect on the company.

MR. PRESIDENT, my notes on the SIXTH SPEAKER'S performance and those who followed him "were confusion worse confounded," for I was so chilled with the coldness of the room, that my fingers would not obey my will-power, and instead of words, when I came to review them, I found naught but hieroglyphics, which would have hopelessly puzzled the decipherer of the hieroglyphics of Thebes and Nineveh, "Champhollion." And when I looked within on the page of memory, I found the entry there in good keeping with my attempted-to-be-notes. But sufficiently enough was legible to enable me to conclude that the effort to make it appear that Riches was the desideratum for the development of character, was a creditable one to the disputant.

He too endowed Milton and Scott with the great prerequisite, money; and it is not to be questioned, that if they possessed the endowment, it did not hinder, but rather helped the former to give to the world his inimitable productions of " Paradise Lost" and Paradise Regained;" and to the latter his world-wide celebrated poem, the " Lady of the Lake," and others equally captivating.

This speaker was calm, collected, and dispassionate; and bids fair, with his well-trained style of reading and speaking, to hold a high position in the elocutionary circle.

The summing up was concise, but hardly full enough in its enumerations of leading arguments which had been advanced to give perspicuity to the discussion, preparatory to the vote. They, however, produced the conviction that they both were in earnest, and also that both believed themselves to be right in their conclusions,—and the Vote that followed showed in the estimation of the Association that both were nearly so.

Have we not, Sir, a striking example of the co-equal influence of Poverty and Riches in developing character in two individuals in the scientific world—Lord Ross and Dr. Lescarbeault? the former giving to science a vast enlargement of astronomical knowledge, resolving doubts and dissolving Nebulæ, and opening up to the mind an almost unlimited field of investigation by his lavish expenditure of wealth to complete that wonderful optical, mathematical instrument by which he peered out into the vast expanse, seemingly approaching the outer confines of vast creation, to catch glimpses of nonentity, where silence and darkness reign undisturbed over the invisible and incomprehensible wastes of Nothingness!

But see in the latter the humble, obscure, and, until quite recently, the almost unknown, poverty-stricken French physician, in a remote inland village in France, with his self-educated mind, his self-erected observatory, his self-manufactured telescope, and other mathematical instruments needful for a correct observation of the heavens; and by husbanding time and means, to enrich our science of the Solar system by adding to it a Ninth primary planet—" Vulcan."

Shall we, or shall we not, Sir, after this discussion, adopt the prayer of Agur, the son of Jakeh, " Give me neither Poverty nor Riches," or shall we pray for both, that all our latent powers may be developed for weal or for woe?

Finally, Sir, your critic would say, that he has listened to a number of discussions as good,—also to many which were worse;—which is greater praise then he anticipates from the Association for his Criticism!

PHRENOLOGY.

"The proper study of mankind is man," was the appropriate remark of the poet-philosopher, and the truth of the assertion is recognized in the fact that the study of mental science has engaged and delighted many of the most gifted of our race in all ages. To sketch but a faint outline of the various systems which have been argued by ingenious projectors with all the eloquence of enthusiasm, but which have successively fallen before the searching glance of critical inquiry, would require much learned research, and would form an extensive library of itself. Many have been the philosophies propounded and admired,—many the absurdities exposed and ridiculed. Here a little, and there a little, of truth has been elicited, but scarcely one system has proved so satisfactory to the mind as to be adopted and adhered to in its entirety, or which has remained steadfast, against the assaults of time.

To establish a system having for its foundation the organic structure of the busy brain itself, was reserved to the great founders of Phrenology,—Gall, Spurzheim, and Combe. It fell to the lot of these gifted men to discover and develop into a science, a system which, though yet comparatively new, is becoming universally recognized, and cannot be studied with attention without furnishing the most incontestible proofs of its conclusiveness; one which reconciles to itself those diversities and anomalies in human character, which give to individuals their peculiar tastes, dispositions, aims and aspirations, and to society its ever changeful aspect.

About the close of the last century Dr. Gall, the first teacher of the new doctrine, endowed with great powers of observation, discovered the *locale* of nearly all the organs known to Phrenology; assisted in his labors and followed by the no less able Dr. Spurzheim, who made valuable additions to its literature.

The new science continued to progress and gain converts among the most discerning men of the time, though not without encountering much bitter opposition from the prejudiced and narrow-minded.

It is to the great Dr. George Combe, however, that the science owes its present form, he having systematized the facts obtained by the two former, and, by his philosophical generalizations, given beauty and harmony to the whole.

Few branches of study can be more interesting to the student, or be rendered more useful to humanity at large, than the study and practice of Phrenological science. And we reccommend its study to all, and especially to the young.

THE END.

www.ingramcontent.com/pod-product-compliance
Lightning Source LLC
Chambersburg PA
CBHW021355230426
43666CB00006B/538